Sr. Maxine Inkel

What Would Jesus Do?

A Catechist's Guide to Discipline

TWENTY-THIRD PUBLICATIONS

185 WILLOW STREET • PO BOX 180 • MYSTIC, CT 06355
TEL: 1-800-321-0411 • FAX: 1-800-572-0788
Bayard   E-MAIL: ttpubs@aol.com • www.twentythirdpublications.com

Scripture quotes are taken from the *New Revised Standard Version Bible*, copyright ©1989, Division of Christian Education of the National Council of the Churches of Christ in the United States of America.

Twenty-Third Publications
A Division of Bayard
185 Willow Street
P.O. Box 180
Mystic, CT 06355
(860) 536-2611
(800) 321-0411
www.twentythirdpublications.com

ISBN:1-58595-201-X
Library of Congress Catelog Card Number: 2002103862
Printed in the U.S.A.

Contents

Introduction

When I hear the word "joy," right away I begin to feel great! One morning a few years ago I was talking on the phone with a friend, telling her how much I love teaching and miss it now that I'm retired. Gwen noted that I have a knack for seeing the bright side of things, even in negative situations.

"That's a gift," she said, "and it's something you should share with catechists and teachers." I thought about that for days. How could I share my joy with those who teach religion?

I transported myself in spirit to my favorite place in the world, the classroom. There I prayed and waited for an idea to come. It did, and the column "From Water to Wine"—which I wrote for *Religion Teacher's Journal*—was the result.

Jesus, as you know, was always teaching. One powerful lesson he taught was at the wedding feast in Cana. He changed water into wine. "Ah," I exclaimed, "I've got it! I know how joy can be brought into a class. It's just a matter of turning the water of negative situations into the wine of joy."

Right away I made a list of situations in a religion class that are definitely "water" (negatives), and I looked for ways to change these into "wine" (positives). Turning water into wine can become a wonderful lifelong habit.

This little book includes most of the material from my original columns. I hope my ideas help and encourage you to look for your own ways to turn difficult situations into joyous, faith-filled ones.

PART ONE

Jesus & Discipline

1

What Would Jesus Do?

What better place to learn about discipline than at the feet of Jesus!

> Jesus called a child, whom he put among them, and said, "Truly I tell you, unless you change and become like children, you will never enter the kingdom of heaven. Whoever becomes humble like this child is the greatest in the kingdom of heaven. Whoever welcomes one such child in my name welcomes me." (Matthew 18:2–5)

In this passage we see how Jesus acts toward children; and our discipline should be inspired by his example. First of all, Jesus gives the child a place of importance. The children we teach are more important than our lesson plans, our personal successes, our schedule, our time, and our feelings.

How does this translate into how we discipline? We know that children want to behave well, want to please us, want to do good work. When they don't want to, there's always a reason. Good discipline demands that we find the reason and address the problem. This may sometimes mean changing our schedule or making a perfect project a little less perfect, but nothing is more important than the child.

We might ask, "What about the other ninety-nine?" (see Mt 18:12–14). Well, we know what Jesus did about the other ninety-nine, don't we? I'm not advocating that we turn the class loose while we comfort a needy child. What I am saying is that we need to evaluate our old approaches to discipline.

A better approach

Let me give a scenario that will show you what I mean. A catechist comes to religion class all fired up about a new project she hopes to begin that day. Things are going along fine until she looks up and sees a child wiping away tears. What's to be done?

Very quietly the catechist changes course. Suppose her project was a skit. The catechist asks one of the children to direct the skit. The project then goes on, while the catechist approaches the unhappy child, smiles, and invites the child to go out and get a drink at the water fountain. The child slips out and the catechist watches the skit from the doorway. When the child returns, the catechist offers whatever emergency help is needed and promises further help later. The child joins the "ninety-nine," and the project continues.

The solution can be as simple as that. That is, it looks simple, but in order to be ready for such events, a catechist needs to have done some remote preparation, such as delegating leadership. Children can learn at a very young age to run a project or class. We need to allow them to do this under our supervision, even when there isn't an emergency.

In the story of Jesus and the children we also notice that Jesus adapts the circumstances to the child, not the other way around. He took the child in his arms. Here's a little child in the midst of a group of big, burly fishermen, who may have been strangers. Such a situation can make a kid feel pretty small. So what does Jesus do? He takes the child in his arms, which brings the child eyeball to eyeball with the men. What a loving gesture on Jesus' part!

What does this say to us as catechists? Even at the sacrifice of our own convenience, we arrange the circumstances in our teaching and in our religion classes to suit the comfort of the children first of all. That involves taking the time to discover the learning styles of the children in order to adapt our teaching style to them. It means being aware of whether or not the chairs fit the children. Adjusting circumstances to suit the child may mean adjusting the room temperature, providing a cracker or cookie, having a sleepy child take a short nap, tying a shoelace, giving a pencil to a child who doesn't have one, and doing everything else we can so our children never feel small, frightened, or embarrassed.

These things may not seem like much, but they can make all the difference in the world in creating a climate conducive to good discipline.

Children are precious

There is one more small point that we can consider in the story of Jesus and the children. Jesus helps us see each child as precious: "Whoever welcomes one such child in my name welcomes me." How do we copy Jesus in this, especially as we look at the discipline situation in our religion classes? All we have to do is see Jesus in each child and act accordingly.

We know that a child with a poor self-image is often a child who will act out to cover up that fact. So, what can we do? We build up that self-image. That's not as hard to do as it seems. Again, it's just a matter of being willing to take the time and make the effort to know the children. In these days of competition and struggle to get to the "top," children often feel so pressured that they don't feel "precious" at all. They feel more like failures who can't seem to please anybody.

How do we deal with that? In simple ways, just as Jesus did. Jesus praised the children to those around him and made the children important in their sight. We can do the same with well-placed praise. We can also actively look for good things the child says or does and praise him/her, and also praise the child to parents, siblings, colleagues, and others—in the presence of the child. Nothing can make a youngster more eager to behave well than having a feeling of true worth.

Let us pray

Jesus, be with us every step of the way during this teaching year. Help us ready our hearts and minds for the changes we may need to make in order to lead the children we teach to you. Amen.

For reflection and discussion

- When you think of classroom discipline, do you think more about how discipline affects you or how it affects the children in your class?

- When disciplinary action becomes necessary (and that only as a last resort!) do you take time to remember the words of Jesus, "Whoever welcomes one such child in my name welcomes me."?

- In carrying out discipline, what is more important to you: your reputation as a good disciplinarian or the feelings of the child involved? What evidence is there of this?

- How can you prepare the climate of your class ahead of time for good discipline? How can you avoid rather than have to remedy discipline problems?

2

Jesus' Compassion

Discipline problems disappear when we imitate the compassion of Jesus.

> [A synagogue leader] named Jairus came and, when he saw Jesus, fell at his feet and begged him repeatedly, "My little daughter is at the point of death. Come and lay your hands on her, so that she may be made well, and live."...While he was still speaking, some people came from the leader's house to say, "Your daughter is dead. Why trouble the teacher any further?" But overhearing what they said, Jesus said to the leader of the synagogue, "Do not fear, only believe." (Mark 5:22–23, 35–36)

In this story, Jesus shows compassion by making short work of the prophets of doom! When the messengers came to announce that the little girl had died, Jesus "ignored them"! How often we have had prophets of doom come to us about a certain child who has a reputation for poor behavior or for lack of concentration. Sometimes these reports come from teachers, sometimes parents, sometimes classmates.

Suppose, for example, that another teacher tells you that a certain child is bad news. How do you ignore this? You could reply, "Thank you for telling me. I'll see what I can do." Or ideally, you know something positive about this child, and you can smile and say, "But I've also heard that this child is a prolific reader." Such a response will tell the other person that you intend to give this child a fair shake and a new start. In a word, you are ignoring the negative reports.

Jesus showed compassion
In the gospel passage, Jairus was crushed about the death of his daughter, and the compassionate Jesus put himself in his shoes. He invited Jairus to help, to *do* something: to get hold of his fear and to believe. "Do not fear, only believe."

Let's say that a child approaches you with an earth-shaking problem, for example, a sudden rain shower has ruined his homework project. The child thinks it's the end of the world. You could give the child a lecture about being more careful or you could be understanding.

If Jesus were faced with this situation, we can imagine what he would do. He would let the child know right away that he or she is a hundred times more important than all the projects in the world. Jesus would probably put his arm around the child while saying, "It's okay! Don't be afraid! We can mend it. It may not look like new, but I can tell that it is a fine project."

Can you imagine how cooperative this child will be the next time you need cooperation? Three months, a year, ten years down the road, what will really be important about that project? Will it be the perfection of it, or how our compassion made a little child feel? We know the answer.

Jesus respected individuals
Let's take one more look at this wonderful story about Jairus and his little daughter. One of the first things Jesus did was to dismiss the crowd, to protect the privacy of the family. Furthermore, the compassionate and selfless Jesus diverted all attention away from his own spectacular action to the needs of the parents. What a lesson for us! Let's face it, at times we

use children to earn accolades for ourselves from other catechists and our DRE. Or we take it out on the children when they make us look bad.

For example, the DRE is visiting your class and the children become nervous, forget the lines they were supposed to recite, and giggle at the most inappropriate times. What do you do? The compassion of Jesus might be the last thing that comes to your mind just then. But, whisper a prayer that Jesus will give you patience and compassion.

When the DRE leaves, tell the children that you understand how it feels to be nervous and that they'll probably do better the next time someone visits. The children will be so relieved at your understanding, they'll assure you that they will do their absolute best the next time.

The story of the ruler's daughter beautifully underscores the compassion of Jesus. We catechists can resolve many of our discipline problems when we approach our children with compassion. Compassion results in happy children, and happy children make for good discipline.

> **Let us pray**
> Jesus, fill our hearts with the same compassion you showed to the people you met each day. May we be an example of kindness and understanding to the children we teach. Amen.

For reflection and discussion
- How do we handle "prophets of doom"? Are you careful not to be a doomsayer yourself?
- How do you handle the small embarrassments or "disasters" in your class? How is your compassion level?
- Are you aware that good discipline depends more on how you act than on how the children act?
- Are you serious about relying on the Master Teacher for the help you need? How do you show this?

3

Jesus the Healer

We are catechists, true. But we can also be healers, especially when it comes to the "problem" children in our religion classes. Here's how.

> As he approached the gate of the town, a man who had died was being carried out. He was his mother's only son, and she was a widow;...When the Lord saw her, he had compassion for her and said to her, "Do not weep." Then he came forward and touched the bier....The dead man sat up and began to speak, and Jesus gave him to his mother. (Luke 7:12–15)

What a story! And what a role model for us catechists. How often, in our classes, we find ourselves in similar situations. We have troubled children in our care. I speak not only of learning-disabled children or of physically handicapped children, but also of those who are striking out at negative situations in their lives (such as poor self-image, inability to make friends, etc.) by behaving badly, a thing no child ever does without a cause. How can we copy Jesus, our role model, in such cases?

First of all, Jesus stops. He is aware of the woman's

suffering. We need to train ourselves in the art of seeing—of being aware, of noticing. We can see a look of anxiety in a child's eyes and face; we can see negative behavior that may not be usual for that child, behavior that has all the earmarks of striking out at something painful; we can see the mannerisms of anxiety or pain or anger, such as breaking a pencil on purpose, or hitting the desk with a fist. With non-demonstrative children, we might see a child sighing, rubbing eyes, or biting nails. Other signs of a hurting child might be inattention or distractibility. All of this is there, but we have to see it—just as Jesus did in the case of the widow.

Offering comfort

The next step in our effort to copy the compassion of Jesus is to offer comfort. A child who is misbehaving because he or she is anxious or hurting doesn't need harsh words or stern discipline from us. Jesus said to the widow in the gospel story, "Do not weep." He doesn't give her a lesson on detachment or on accepting God's will.

It's true that often behind bad behavior is a weeping child. A gentle smile, a little extra help with a task, some small gesture of attention will let this child know that our doors and our hearts are open. Then, as Jesus did, we can use healing words like "I notice that you're a little upset today. Would you like to talk about it? Maybe I can help."

A third way we can imitate the compassion of Jesus is by action. He touched the bier. He ordered the young man to arise, and he returned him to his mother. It has to be the same with us. We need to follow our words with concrete action. Some of the actions we might take include letting the child express the awfulness of the event in his or her life (a hurt shared is a hurt minimized); depending upon the situation, we might suggest some coping skills; or we might arrange to meet with both child and parent. (Such a meeting could possibly save a child from much unnecessary suffering or at least open the door to communication between the child and his or her parents.)

As a busy catechist, you might say, "Hey, I don't have time for this sort of thing!" Well, Jesus, our role model, took time for this sort of thing; and, after all, it really doesn't take that much more time or effort to really see, to reach out, and to follow through. It's especially worth it if it helps you solve the discipline problems caused by deep hurts in the children you teach.

We can bring compassionate healing to all the discipline situations in our classrooms by recalling how Jesus dealt with the widow: 1) he was aware; 2) he gave comfort; 3) he added action to his words.

Let us pray

Compassionate Jesus, please help us to deal in a compassionate way with the discipline problems in our classes by studying how you dealt with difficult situations. Teach me to see the problems, to comfort the child, and to follow my words with action. Help me to imitate you. Amen.

For reflection and discussion

- Are you adequately prepared to meet the needs of children who have problems? Do you take time daily for a little extra professional reading?

- Are you in the habit of solving discipline problems from a psychological viewpoint only, or do you operate from a faith-base, seeking guidance in prayer and in the example of Jesus? Do you teach children to solve problems from a faith-base?

4

Jesus Answers a Call for Help

Just as Jesus helped and healed the leper in Mark's gospel, we too are called to help heal our own disruptive youngsters.

Most of us know by now that a child who has a discipline problem is a child who is in need of something. Usually a child's negative behavior is a call for help. If we imitate Jesus, our response will be swift and all-accepting, full of compassion. Like Jesus, we will let our little ones know by our words and actions that we want to help and heal them. The following story of Jesus and the leper gives us added insights and inspiration.

A leper came to him begging him, and kneeling he said to him, "If you choose, you can make me clean." Moved with pity, Jesus stretched out his hand and touched him, and said to him, "I do choose. Be made clean!" (Mark 1:40–41)

One of the primary lessons from this story is the example of Jesus' compassion and acceptance of the leper—just as he was. We catechists can hardly help crying out, "Oh, I wish I could be like that!" The wonder is that we can be like that! In fact, we need to be.

It is not difficult for us to identify some of the little "lepers" in our classes. Their call for help cries out to us through their negative behavior. Our very attitude goes a long way toward helping a disruptive child. That attitude consists in our not seeing that child as a troublemaker, but as a child calling out to us, "If you will, you can help me!" We see that Jesus doesn't say, "Yuck! A leper! I'm outta here!" On the contrary, he "stretches out his hand and touches the leper."

Reaching out as Jesus did
We too are stretching out our hands to our little children every time we make an effort to find out why they are acting out. We can do this in several ways:

First of all, we can try not to pre-judge. By engaging a disruptive child in conversation in a private, non-threatening guidance session, we can usually find out what the child's agenda is. Perhaps we have interpreted certain behaviors in too negative a manner. Perhaps the child is tired or slow to comprehend, can't see well or hear well. In such situations you will want to let the child know that you care and are willing to offer your time and help. Most of the time this works, and you will indeed find out what is bothering the child.

Another approach is to ask a disruptive child to help you with routine tasks. This says to the child: "I trust you. You're OK. I know I can expect good things of you." You might also want to take the time needed to look into the child's background and family situation, consult permanent records, and/or speak to former teachers and DREs. This could give you insight into possible causes for poor behavior.

When you have all the information you need, first pray for help and then set about addressing the problems. You will soon see marked improvement in the behavior of your youngster, and best of all you will be walking in the footsteps of Jesus.

Another thing you might find helpful is to ask the child to make a list for you of things that make him or her happy. (When I was less experienced, I used to ask children to make a list of things that made them unhappy. I discovered that even though this led me more quickly to the information I sought, the practice opened wounds for some children. Nothing was worth that!) If you can read between the lines, you will discover from the child's list of "happy things" hints about what might be upsetting the child.

If these approaches don't work, or if you're dealing with especially bad behavior, try to find time to meet with the child one-on-one. Welcome the child with a smile and say: "I noticed that you were having problems with behavior today, and I have an idea. Would you like to pray with me about this?" Then, have a spontaneous session of prayer that includes prayers like "Help me to..." and "Thank you for..." and "I'm sorry for..." and "I'll try harder to...." At the end of the session, thank the child for trying harder. Remember, it's Jesus' method we're using!

Let us pray

Jesus, you who stretched out your hand and touched the leper, please touch our hearts and inspire in us a great desire to accept others as you do. Bless the children we teach, especially those who are difficult to deal with. May we be a loving, forgiving, and healing presence in their lives. Amen.

For reflection and discussion

- Remember the quote in the film *Pollyanna* that changed the minister's outlook? "If we look for the bad in a person, we will surely find it." Do you tend to jump to conclusions about certain children in your religion class? Do you try to see the best in each child?

- Do you make time to meet with each child, especially when there is a behavior problem?

- How often do you praise your youngsters when they do well, even if it's for something small?

5

Jesus Sees Us
as Unique Persons

In passage after passage of the gospel we read that Jesus was followed by the crowd, was surrounded by people who wanted to hear and touch him. Let's look at how Jesus dealt with crowds (groups) and learn from him how to handle "crowds" in our religion classes, not as a faceless cluster of children, but as a gathering of precious individuals made in the image and likeness of God. Let's begin, then, with a gospel story about Jesus and a crowd.

The woman who was healed

As Jesus went, the crowds pressed in on him. Now there was a woman who had been suffering from hemorrhages for twelve years; and though she had spent all she had on physicians, no one could cure her. She came up behind him and touched the fringe of his clothes, and immediately her hemorrhage stopped. Then Jesus asked, "Who touched me?" When all denied it, Peter said, "Master, the crowds surround you and press in on you."

But Jesus said, "Someone touched me; for I noticed that power had gone out from me." When the woman saw that she could not remain hidden, she came trembling; and falling down before him, she declared in the presence of all the people why she had touched him, and how she had been immediately healed. He said to her, "Daughter, your faith has made you well; go in peace." (Luke 8:42–48)

The woman was one in a crowd, but Jesus wanted to encounter her on a personal level, to speak words of comfort. There are other examples of the "personal touch" Jesus brought to his ministry.

Jesus went about teaching

What does it mean to teach? Webster says that it means "to show how (and we might add: to show who) and to give knowledge of." A good way "to show who" when it comes to Jesus, is to make sure that we show him to ourselves, first and often, by spending quality time with our New Testament and with solid reading about Jesus. It's much the same with the second part of the definition: "to give knowledge of." Once we ourselves have grown in our knowledge of Jesus, we'll be more ready and able to impart this knowledge to each child in our religion class.

One of the best ways to teach about Jesus and his message is to involve children in the lesson (which is also one of the best ways to keep good discipline—active and involved children don't have time for mischief). So, involve children by telling them stories about Jesus from the gospels and let them role-play these.

After sharing a number of stories in this way, invite children to choose their favorite story. Then give each child a sheet of 8" x 11" manila paper and have them fold the paper in half. On the top, ask them to draw a picture of their Jesus story and on the bottom have them draw themselves "doing as Jesus did" in a contemporary setting. When the drawings are complete, have a sharing session so children can show and explain their drawings. When youngsters see that you and others are really listening to them, they will be less inclined to "act up" for attention.

Jesus went about preaching

Yes, as laborers in the vineyard of Jesus, we too are involved in preaching. You might think: "Me? I can't preach!" But, of course, you can and do preach all day long by what you say and how you act, how you treat each child. You also preach in religion class whenever you talk about and give witness to Jesus. In this sense, children too can be preachers, especially if we show them how to proclaim Jesus by our words and actions.

To make this more concrete, ask the children what changes they would like to see in the world or in their neighborhoods, in their families, in their classes at school, or in themselves. List the "changes" on the board or on a poster.

Then, working in small groups, have the children look through the New Testament to find a story about something Jesus did that they, too, can do to change our world for the better. For example, let's say that the change needed is "to be more grateful for the good things people do." The story Jesus told about the widow giving her last coin to the temple collection is a good example. (See Luke 21:1–4) We find that 1) Jesus noticed what the poor widow did, and 2) he praised her to those around him.

Ask children: can we do something like this? Of course they can, and here's one way. Make a list with the children of all the kind deeds they have seen people (including their classmates) do lately. Then discuss whether or not anyone has shown appreciation for these actions. If not, encourage the children to show their appreciation by thanking the person themselves, either in person or by mail. In this small way, they will be preaching right alongside Jesus. You may want to give the example by talking about the good things or gifts/talents (however small) each child in your group has brought to the class.

Jesus went about healing

In our story about Jesus and the crowd, Jesus goes about healing. To "heal" means "to cure" and "to mend." Here's a simple way to illustrate the meaning of healing for children.

Without any prior explanation, begin making a fence with "fence posts" on either a bulletin board or felt board. The fence posts can be made by cutting out large strips of paper or felt and making one end pointed. Put in one fence post at a time slowly until you have the complete attention of your class. Then, oops! pin one strip as if the fence post has fallen over. Explain that this fence is a symbol of our lives. Very often we allow negative things to keep our fence from being nice and straight and steady. Discuss what these negative things might be, for example: selfishness, unwillingness to forgive, prejudice, spite, name-calling, disobedience, etc. (Note: This might be a good time to talk to children about an examination of conscience in preparation for the sacrament of reconciliation.)

Now, list qualities that help us to "mend" or heal the fence. For example: thinking of others, unselfishness, forgiveness, acceptance of differences, etc. Then straighten your fallen-over "fence-post." This simple activity illustrates that all of us have weaknesses that can be healed, and often we are healed with the help of others. As followers of Jesus, we too can heal others by our good example and support. And, of course, we can each count on God's love for healing—no matter what needs "mending."

Let us pray

Thank you, Jesus, for all that you teach us as we follow your footsteps through the gospels. Help us to imitate the way you taught, preached, and healed, that we too might be proclaimers of God's kingdom to the little ones entrusted to our care. Amen.

For reflection and discussion

- When you stand before the children in your class, do you see just a sea of faces or do you see individual little "masterpieces" of God—unique persons with their own gifts and quirks?

- When you feel harassed and helpless, for whatever reason, are you able to ask for help from your DRE or principal—and from God through prayer?

- Are there areas in your teaching that could use a good dose of compassion and understanding? Do you pray often for these gifts?

6

Jesus Empowers Others

Just as Jesus would never embarrass one of his followers, so we should never embarrass those we teach. This calls for a great deal of compassion—and the ability to make children feel good about themselves, as Jesus did.

> When they reached Capernaum, the collectors of the temple tax came to Peter and said, "Does your teacher not pay the temple tax?" He said, "Yes, he does." And when he came home, Jesus spoke of it first, asking, "What do you think, Simon? From whom do kings of the earth take toll or tribute? From their children or from others?" When Peter said, "From others," Jesus said to him, "Then the children are free. However, so that we do not give offense to them, go to the sea and cast a hook; take the first fish that comes up; and when you open its mouth, you will find a coin; take that and give it to them for you and me." (Matthew 17:24–27)

This story is a treasure-chest of great ideas for us as we struggle to achieve good, compassionate, effective discipline in our classes. Let's have a look at several of these ideas.

1) Jesus spoke first. Jesus didn't wait for Peter to ask for his

help. He broke the ice and put Peter at ease. This teaches us catechists that often a discipline problem can be averted by our simply being aware of another's need.

This is an acquired skill and the first step toward acquiring it is prayer. We become familiar with the ways of Jesus only through faithful, daily scriptural prayer. Second, we make sure that we are well acquainted with the basis of good psychology and child development and remember that discipline problems are always the result of some underlying cause. Children seldom misbehave because they want to. They misbehave because something is off kilter in their lives. Our job is to do what Jesus did with Peter: be aware of the signs and discover and address the problem before it blows up!

We have to recognize that distress and frustration are signs that a child needs help. A simple question is sometimes all it takes to solve an issue.

2) Jesus involved Peter in decision making. "Hey, Peter, what do you think?" We can do the same in our classes when confronted with situations that cause discipline problems. We can find ways to involve the child in the solution to the problem. Rather than saying, "Now, here's what we're going to do!" we can say, "Do you have any ideas on how we can solve this problem?" Even if the child hasn't a clue, he or she will feel good about being asked, and together you will more easily come up with a solution.

3) Jesus empowered Peter. He didn't say, "Bring the money to me and I'll pay the tax." He told Peter, you do it! This showed that Jesus knew Peter well. He probably smiled at what he knew would happen. Peter would dash up to the money-takers with a didn't-I-tell-you-so look on his face, and plunk the money on the table.

It's hard to delegate power in a classroom. I know. I've been there. But, if we want to have good discipline, the effort has to be collaborative. If we try to impose discipline from on high, the children may behave for the moment, but if we take our eyes off of them, they will explode like firecrackers and find ways to escape our control.

Scripture doesn't say so, but I suspect that this experience taught the impetuous Peter lessons that no doubt proved valuable in his later ministry. He had many opportunities to speak first to save others from embarrassment; to involve others in decisions that had to be made; and to empower others as they struggled to preach the gospel.

Before I leave this story I'd like to make a suggestion. Why not find some way to share the ideas we glean from stories about Jesus with parents to help them achieve good discipline in the home, too. There is much they can learn from the respect and compassion of Jesus.

Let us pray

Gentle Jesus, Lord of compassion, you treated the impetuous Peter with thoughtfulness and selflessness. And thus you helped him to grow in faith and in goodness. Please help us to achieve good discipline in our classes by imitating you. May those we teach also grow in faith and goodness. Amen.

For reflection and discussion

- Do you involve the children in finding solutions to a problem? Why or why not? How can you improve in this area?

- Have I let the children collaborate in formulating the rules of behavior for religion class, as well as the consequences for breaking one of the rules?

- Do I delegate tasks often and impartially, with consideration for the feelings and abilities of each child?

PART TWO

From Water to Wine

7

When You Can't Get Their Attention

Don't know what to do with all the "energy" in your class? Apply these suggestions for teaching the faith to the fidgety.

It takes just one well-situated domino to knock down all the rest. Just so, it takes only one distractible child to create chaos in your class—even if everyone else and everything else is in perfect order. (Note that I could say "disruptive," but distractible sounds more fair to the child.) An inexperienced catechist might ask, "How will I know if I have a distractible child in my class?" An experienced catechist will reply, "You won't be able to miss 'em!"

What does that experienced catechist know about a distractible child? Let's examine some of the signs. A distractible child, finds it hard to sit still, to concentrate on one thing, to make decisions. The child roams around the room aimlessly, talks out at inappropriate times, requires inordinate amounts of your attention, seldom completes a task, makes rhythmic sounds with pencils, crayons, whatever. Plus, this child finds it hard to follow directions, especially oral or complex ones.

How soon will you know whether God has blessed you with a distractible child? During the first two minutes of your very first class! What does a catechist do? First of all, as with all difficult situations, a catechist can pray: "Jesus, I'm not really sure how to handle this. Please be at my side, guiding me as to how to lead this child to you."

It helps to know 1) the reasons for the child's lack of attention and 2) the techniques for easing the situation.

Getting to know them

If the children are in first to third grades (or younger), there are just certain basics about that age level. We know that little bodies are still growing and require movement. This is also an age of curiosity, so necessary for learning. For example, if a child sees a beetle on the windowsill, he has to go see it up close! That means he's out of his seat and has distracted the group, right? Other children may have to deal with ADD or ADHD—Attention Deficit Hyperactivity Disorder. Still others may become restless because of a learning disability that makes reading difficult. You may want to obtain professional advice in working with these children.

How do we redirect everyone's attention? Well, we can spend fifteen minutes yelling, or we can stop, comment on the wonder of a beetle and, perhaps, even tie the event to the teaching material at hand. Then, in good environmental fashion, we can have someone take the beetle outdoors to freedom. Simple, isn't it? (You might think "Hey, if I give that much attention to an old beetle, the children will start planting creepy-crawlers all over the room, and that will be the living end of learning anything!" No! No! That'll only happen if your class is so boring that it deserves creepy-crawlers!)

The payoff is that when you are ready to get back to your subject, the children will follow like you are the Pied Piper because they will have identified you as a person of compassion and understanding. Besides, it's Jesus' way!

Teaching techniques

When working with young children, lesson plans need to include the kind of teaching that has children out of their seats more than in them. Let me explain. Let's say you are at a review point. You could just go around the room asking questions and expecting memorized answers. Or you could try a different approach.

Let's suppose that the test asks for fill-in-the-blanks. You can tell the children, "If you know the word that fills in that blank, stand up, turn around once in your spot, sit back down and write in the answer. If we're quiet enough, we can do the whole review like this." That way, your review gets done and the physical needs of the children are met. Easy, isn't it?

As for memorizing, there are many fun ways to do that. One might be this: Tell the children you are going to recite what needs to be remembered by them. When you raise your hand, the children say the missing word, phrase, or sentence. By making it a game, you'll be able to go over the material until they can say it on their own. Children love games and motion, so you'll definitely have their attention.

You might also want to use puppets (a happy face taped onto a ruler or yardstick will work). Have two children operate the puppets in this way: One puppet asks a question, the other puppet answers in his or her own words. Then, one puppet "forgets" (on purpose!) and has to be "prompted" by the class. Children love this. Attention won't be a problem, but holding down the volume on the "prompters" might be.

Another tremendous help is to have a *carrel* in your room. You can make one from a large box (one that fits on a desk or small table in your meeting space). Cut out one side of the box, set it on the table and you have your carrel. What's the value of a carrel? It cuts down space for a distractible child and makes it easier for the child to concentrate on the work at hand.

Once your carrel is set up, your next concern is to make the child's work as colorful and as interesting as possible in order to center his/her attention on it. In fact, making work interesting is a good idea for your whole class.

Another help for distractible children is to place them close to you in lecture-type situations or when you're reading a story or giving directions. When you give directions, remember that usually a distractible child cannot handle multiple directions. Even single directions must be given slowly, clearly, and with as few words as possible. Again, giving directions this way is good for any child, at any time.

Distractible children are liable to just get up and roam at the most inappropriate times. Something has caught their attention. There's one simple solution for this. At some time outside of class, make a pact with the children, telling them that when you say a code word, like K-13 or 3-D or whatever, that means they are to return to home base. This should be done like a game and not embarrass the children. If you have activities that keep your youngsters "on the move" regularly, distractible children will have fewer problems with roaming.

When children talk out, require too much of your attention, or play drums on their desks with pencils, just edge over to them and place your hand gently on their hand and smile. The child will smile back and get the idea.

Finishing tasks

A distractible child will have trouble finishing tasks. That doesn't have to be a problem for you either. You have various options.

- You can team the child up with another child who can help her or him stay on task. When you choose this option, it's a good idea to set up more than one team so that the child won't feel "different" or "singled out."

- You can adjust the child's task, if necessary, having the child do just enough of the assignment to let you know that she or he has grasped the content. Again, it's ideal if you can do this for several of the children and not just one. One way to adjust an assignment would be to prepare more than one worksheet. On one sheet would be the regular assignment, on another would be the same assignment but in a much shorter and simpler form. The worksheets would be given out at random, making sure distractible children receive the simpler version. Or, you might use the same worksheet for everyone and mark the few items you want the children to do.

- A third way to keep the children on task is to make sure that you are often close by to see what they are doing. This can be done quite naturally without singling out any one child. Just ask how many items are finished or if they need help. These simple gestures bring the children back to task. Again, this is what we should be doing for all the children, but in the case of the distractible child it has to be done more often.

It isn't easy being a distractible child. Just think how often the child is scolded or punished by well-meaning persons who don't understand that the child can't help being distracted. When you see that child's grateful smile in your class because you have done a few simple things to make life easier for him or her, you will feel blessed.

And remember how pleased Jesus will be: "Just as you did it to one of the least of these who are members of my family, you did it to me" (Matthew 25:40). Jesus might even make up a new beatitude for you: "Blessed are those who have taken the pressure off distractible children, for heaven is surely theirs!"

Let us pray
Jesus, gentle Teacher, may many teachers— including me—be willing to do the little things that need to be done so that learning about their faith may be enjoyable for all your children, especially those easily distracted. Give me patience and love for every child I teach. Amen.

For reflection and discussion

- What techniques and approaches have you used in teaching a distractible child? Which have worked best for you and why?

- Try some of the activities suggested in this chapter and discuss the results with other catechists.

8

When It's Just Too Quiet!

Silence may be golden, but not all the time!

Occasionally I've met catechists whose problem isn't with overactive, distractible children. Instead their youngsters are unusually quiet and subdued. Ordinarily, we catechists and teachers are looking for ways to peel the children off the ceiling so that we can quiet them down enough to teach them a little something. But if we look at the variety in God's creation, is it so surprising to find such differences in children?

I can't remember any teacher-training courses titled "How to Handle Quiet Classes"—can you? However, because we have been trained to respect and appreciate differences in individual children, I believe that it is possible to apply to our classes what we have learned about individualization.

The shortest way to success in any religion class is to get the Master Teacher, Jesus, involved. After quiet prayer in the Divine Presence we can relax and listen. You can plan on it, there will be a response and you will know what to do.

Looking for reasons
If you have ultra-quiet children, one thing you need to do is to find the reason for the unusual situation. You may be

dealing with a severely repressed group. In that case, you will want to continue with the activities you are using, being aware that it will take time to convince these children that, in your class, it's acceptable and even preferable for them to feel free to use the motor activities and exhibit the lively behavior of children their age. After five or six classes you should be able to discern whether you are dealing with a repressed group of children or not.

On the other hand, you might just have a class that is quiet by nature.

In order to get the "feel" of the children in your class, study them. Do they seem passive and unhappy with no sparkle in their eyes, and just intent on getting through class only "'cause they hafta"? Or, does the "quiet" seem to suit the children? Do they seem comfortable with it?

Encouraging expression

If it's the first case, and your class is quiet and subdued because of prior repression, do all you can to spark them up again. Take your class outdoors on a nice day and practice shouting for joy at such a lovely day yelling, "Thank you, God!" In the classroom, continue to encourage the children to express their thoughts. It will help if you can praise any appropriate form of participation and liveliness.

Choose Scripture passages and/or parables that are joyful and try getting the children to read them orally with pizzazz! If they hesitate, show them how! Go overboard if you have to.

Now, let's say that your "study" of your class reveals the fact that the children are just quiet by nature and like it that way. Exuberance and pizzazz won't do; like Jesus you'll have to adapt yourself to their needs. Remember Nicodemus and Zacchaeus and how differently Jesus treated each? (See John 3 and Luke 19.) He allowed Nicodemus to come to him quietly by night, but to Zacchaeus, the gregarious one, Jesus shouted, "Hey! Zacchaeus! Come down off that limb because we are going to celebrate at your house today!"

Adapting as Jesus did

Like Jesus, we too have to adapt. When our classes are gregarious, we plan "Hurray!" activities. When our classes are quiet, we lead them to the knowledge of Jesus quietly. Some of the things we can do with a quiet class might include reading Scripture meditatively; introducing the children to sacred art; reading or writing poetry; initiating the children to soul-quieting chant; treating them to short periods of silent time before the eucharistic Jesus. With a little effort all of these can be fitted into the material in your scope-and-sequence chart for the year.

Do we use physical activities with these quiet children? Oh, yes! All children need games and motion, but these, too, must be adapted to the children's quiet nature. With a gregarious class, start class on All Saints Day with a march outdoors (weather permitting, of course!), bellowing "O When the Saints Go Marching In." With a quiet group, though, it would make more sense to have the children walk around the room while you play a quiet hymn. That would still be taking care of the children's physical needs.

So, although heaven knows your situation is indeed unusual, it is possible to adapt to it with the help of our Master Teacher and a few techniques geared to your particular group of children.

Let us pray

Jesus, Master Teacher, I have a different kind of class this year. Please help me adapt to these children as you so compassionately adapt to each of us. Amen.

For reflection and discussion

- If you have a whole group of, ultra-quiet children, have you tried to determine the reason why they are subdued?

- What steps have you taken to 1) help the children enjoy religion class; 2) adapt to their comfort level if that means being more subdued?

- What works best with your youngsters?

9

When Children
Hurt One Another

A catechist once wrote to me about a girl in her seventh grade class who was the butt of whispered jokes. The catechist was asking me for advice on how to handle the problem.

Her situation is a common one, unfortunately, and it is heart-breaking. Perhaps the reason we feel so strongly about this situation is that we all probably have experienced similar treatment at some time or other, and we know in our hearts how awful it feels. My friend's situation is more painful because of the particular age group, where acceptance is so crucial.

So, what's to be done? As always, help is available and close at hand either in the prayer area in your home or before Jesus in the Blessed Sacrament in your parish adoration chapel.

Then, what's to be done in class? First of all, we have to know why this is going on. To do that we observe. What are we looking for?

What to look for

About the children doing the hurting, we need to know: do they feel inferior in some way to the girl, causing them to want to bring her down? a little jealous, maybe? Is the girl being taunted a recent arrival to the class, seen as a threat to well-established cliques? Is she of a different social class or ethnic background? Are the other children afraid of her for some reason and, therefore, inclined to reinterpret the Golden Rule to read, "Do unto others before they do unto you?"

About the girl being victimized, we need to know: does she have mannerisms or some character trait that annoy others? For example, is she so desperate for acceptance that she is seen as cloying? Is she arrogant? Is she actually superior to the others and more than eager to let them know it? Or is she mousy, inviting ridicule?

It could be all of those things or none of them; but, no matter what, something has to be done. Group/class projects can often help open children's eyes to a new point of view, a new understanding. Let's look at a couple you might try.

A project for Thanksgiving

Tell your students that for a whole day (or week) you will ask them to think about and observe someone in the class about whom they might find it difficult to give thanks. They are to look for the good things in that other person. (Include yourself in the project, if you feel comfortable doing it.) In the next class, give each child a sheet of paper (or construction paper or whatever) and have them fold it in half. (No names will be used.) On the top half of the paper, have them describe the person as they used to see him or her. On the bottom half, have the children describe something in that person that they can really thank God for.

This may not seem like much, but it's a beginning. This simple activity may help your students exclaim, "Hey! Maybe there's more to that person than meets the eye!"

An Advent chain

Have each of the children cut out strips of paper to be made into a link-chain. Suggest that all of you concentrate during this Advent on "building up" the class by acts of kindness and/or helpfulness (done in secret, if possible). As each kind deed is done, a link is added to the chain. You might want to propose, as an additional way to please God, that you all do the first acts of kindness for the persons you like least. The acts of kindness might be as simple as giving a compliment, saying a prayer for the person, spending time with that person, choosing that person as a teammate in a project, whatever.

The chain can be kept in a special prayer place in each child's home, and at night prayers they can add the link(s). Then on Christmas Eve, during private prayer time, the children can offer this chain as a gift to Jesus. The only responsibility for the catechist in this very private project is to remind the children at each class that the project is going on.

What will this accomplish? Well, hopefully, with the help of God, this simple project will make classmates aware of the good points of the persons at the bottom of their "caring list," and perhaps, stop the persecution in the situation you mention.

The problem of children hurting one another is a serious one. If left unresolved it could result in a lifetime of bad memories for all involved. The few ideas I've given here may be of some help; they may be expanded and adapted to your needs. You can also count on the help of our loving God to touch hearts and teach kindness.

Let us pray

Jesus, Master-Teacher, you experienced rejection and ridicule in your lifetime. You know how horrible it feels. Please help my class and me to eradicate any kind of meanness among us, so that no child be hurt by this kind of thing in our class, ever again. Amen.

For reflection and discussion

- Have you had to deal with children who hurt one another in your religion class? How did you handle the situation?

- Discuss with other catechists some of the suggestions and points made in this chapter. What has worked for them? for you? What other ideas can you come up with?

10

When a Child Has an Attitude

You know the scenario. It may be only one boy or girl involved...or a few. Their comments in class about the topics you are studying are more remarks than participation, usually negative and always distracting. Perhaps they delight in "pushing your buttons." How can you turn this "water" into "wine"? Tap into the power of the Spirit. Following serious prayer for this student, we observe! It could be that his "negative and distracting remarks" have nothing at all to do with you, your class, or the subject.

What's at the root?
It is entirely possible that you are dealing with a hurting child who, perhaps, is unable to react to the actual source of his hurt, and is striking out at whatever else is at hand. Are there family problems that are impacting this child negatively? Is this, perhaps, a neglected youngster who is looking for the attention he doesn't get at home? Does this student have a poor self-image which he tries to cover up with bravado? Does

this youngster have any particular learning difficulties that have never been addressed?

You might also consider whether it is possible that the youngster's background in religious education is so deficient that nothing in your class interests him or makes any sense to him, because he doesn't have the proper preparation for your class. It could be that this kid hasn't a clue about who Jesus is, let alone what the Trinity or the Holy Spirit are about.

These are some of the questions that may need to be asked. You may think of others.

Coping constructively

Once you have established the probable cause of the problem, the next step is to find ways to address it. Let's suppose that what you have is a neglected child. If this turns out to be the case, you might want to try something like this: as you go over the lesson, keep this youngster in mind, and address his/her needs, anonymously, in that context.

For example, let's say you are preparing the children for the celebration of confirmation and today you are studying the gift of fortitude. You might talk about instances in which a person's life circumstances are difficult, unfair, and negative, for example, belonging to a home in which parents either do not have time for the kids or simply do not take time, leaving the children to fend for themselves. You can show that the gift of fortitude can help children cope with this in constructive ways: doing something creative and kind for friends, neighbors or family, thus growing in kindness and fulfilling the need to belong.

The ideal would be to involve the children's parents in addressing the problem, and see if something can be done. It's true that parents are sometimes unaware that there is a problem.

Learning difficulties

On the other hand, if children have difficulties in some area of learning, one solution might be tutoring. Another would be providing opportunities in class for the children to succeed, and then giving them due praise. An individualized program for these youngsters might be the answer. This may take a little more of your time, but it would be worth it.

If the problem is deficient preparation, then again an individualized program would be a possibility; or you might do your class reviews with these children in mind. Other options are: see that the children are enrolled in a class that is teaching material they need to know, or team them up with a retired catechist in the parish who can help the youngsters develop their faith life.

If the children are simply not ready for the sacrament of confirmation, it might benefit everyone for them to wait awhile. In this case, all those involved—children, parents, pastor, administrators—would need to meet and decide on the best way to effect a delay. One helpful thing to remember is that a child doesn't do negative things because he/she enjoys it. There's always a reason—always!

We might ask also: do we in some way encourage this behavior by giving it too much attention? Does the reaction of other youngsters give these children an incentive to continue this negative behavior? When the children act out, do they seem a little cocky and proud of themselves, or are their eyes sad or angry or have that please-help-me look?

Non-directive counseling
You might want to use a little non-directive counseling with them. Here's one way to do it. Ask to meet with each child and arrange your meeting on "eye-level." Here's what I mean by that: both of you sit in student desks or at a table or on a picnic bench or any place other than with you at a teacher's desk and the child on a chair nearby. This last arrangement is designed, it seems to me, to clam-up rather than open the heart of a child. It's too much of an I'm-big-and-you're-little-situation. It doesn't work.

At your meeting, have a mint or two or a cookie or some such thing as ice-breakers. Both of you can chomp a bit before the session begins. You might say something like this: "I've noticed that you like to participate in class a lot. Where did you learn to do that?"

Then, be pleasant, smile, relax, and *wait*. The real success of non-directive counseling depends upon the teacher's ability to wait, wait, wait! We can't be afraid of long periods of silence. It only seems as if nothing is going on. While you wait, this child is actually identifying you, deciding if he or she can trust your patience and kindness, wondering what you're up to, and little by little letting go. Just *wait!* Trust me. It's worth it.

Eventually, the child will either answer your question or change the subject and begin talking about something else. It's in these "something-elses" that you will find clues on how to work with this child. You may find out how the child feels about the class, individual children, you, family, self.

After that, it will be easy to know what to do. If it's a problem with the other children or you, that is easily addressed. If it's a family problem, you may have to do a little parent counseling, too. If youngsters feel inadequate about themselves, you can use their very behavior to give them a sense of worth through participation that is positive instead of negative.

Let us pray
Spirit of God, I'm concerned about _____. I don't seem to be able to understand or help him/her. I ask for an infusion of your gifts, especially wisdom and understanding for both of us. Amen.

For reflection and discussion

- When you have a child with a negative attitude, how can you discover what's at the root of it, without compromising the child's privacy?

- What steps can you take (or have you taken)? Have you tried non-directive counseling? How has it worked for you?

11

When You Face Small Group Chaos

Have you ever experienced this? You begin small group work with your children; you give directions and assign tasks. Within a few minutes no one seems to know what they're doing, and chaos results. What do you do?

To start with, permit me to give a few ideas about grouping. One of the techniques I used for forming the groups consists in the following. Have a set of small cards with the children's names on them. Your own name will always be at the bottom of the pile. Then, place large, colorful numbers around the rooms to fit the number of groups you'll need to accommodate the number of children in your class. Shuffle your name-cards and call out the name of the child whose name-card lands on the top of the pile. That child then goes to the area with one of the numbers on it. Call the next name and so on. When one group is filled, the children choose from groups that are still available. You do that until all names are called.

Few-write-simplify

Now that we have the children in groups, what then? Here are some key words to remember: few-write-simplify. Let's develop these key words:

Few. This refers to giving as few oral directions at a time as possible. True, some children can follow several directions at a time, but most can't handle more than one or two at a time. If you give too many directions, either the children will forget the directions, or arguments take place as to the order of the directions. Whichever the case, chaos ensues! It's good to know that this can be avoided, simply by working with the wonderful senses God gave us.

That leads me to our second key word: *Write.* When we give the directions orally, that engages the sense of hearing. To help the children, we can use a second sense: sight. We can write the directions on the board, on large sheets of newsprint, or on a sheet for each group. If your children are easily distracted, it wouldn't hurt to give each child a set of directions, and have them point to the directions as you read them.

Simplify. In the case of directions for small group work, it's crucial to cut the number of words to a bare minimum, and to make the form of the directions such that the children don't need to dive for a dictionary or thesaurus to know what the directions say. So, the key here is simplicity both in vocabulary and in the number of words.

Besides the key words, there are other little things that are helpful. For example, even though you work with one of the groups (mostly as an observer), you will need to have a "roving eye" over the whole class—ready to arbitrate if things flare up, as they probably will.

As to choice of group leaders, it is sometimes good to have children choose their own, if they are mature enough. If you choose or assign them, again you might want to do it by name-cards, so that no partiality be shown, and also that all children, whether they are natural leaders or not, get a chance to lead.

Your preliminary directions should include 1) the aim of the discussion, 2) time limits, and 3) the form for reporting. At some point, then, we will need to teach them how to summarize and report. This doesn't have to be complicated, really. One way to teach this skill is an exercise like this: read a short poem, or a short paragraph, or tell a joke. Have the children jot down key words as you go along. Then, ask volunteers to retell what they heard. This, by the way, is also good memory training.

What are some of the advantages of training children at an early age to learn how to participate in small group discussion? I believe that it is a lifetime skill we need. Also, small group work favors those who may have wonderful ideas which they will share in a small group, but won't venture to share in a large one. Another advantage of small group work in religion class: it is easier for all the children to participate, whereas if your group is large, there are time constraints that prevent total participation.

Let us pray
Jesus, Master Catechist, help me learn from you the best ways for communicating your message to the children I teach. May your Spirit guide my words and actions to be simple, few, but effective. Give me your wisdom. Amen.

For reflection and discussion
- How often do you engage the children in your class in small group work? What are some of the pros and cons?
- What type of group work do your youngsters enjoy most, e.g., games, crafts, discussions?
- What are some of the skills (social, emotional, spiritual) that small group work can help children develop?

12

When You Face Post-Vacation Jitters

After vacation and at the end of the school year, it's so much more difficult to catch and keep the attention of the children in our religion classes. It's good to remember that when our youngsters return from vacation we need to let them slow down gradually and not expect them to go from vacation to work—Pow! just like that! They can't do it!

Easing re-entry with activity

So, you ease them in by making sure that their re-entry is full of activity as well as learning. For example, if the re-entry is after spring break, the children may come into your classroom full of springtime and wanting to be anywhere in the world except in your class. So, you can begin class with what I like to call an "active-prayer." Play lively prayer music such as "He's Got the Whole World in His Hands" or "Michael, Row the Boat Ashore." Or if it's close to Easter, listen to one of the booming hymns of Easter that whoop it up over the fact that Jesus our Lord is risen, Alleluia!

As the music plays, the children (and you) can march around the room (or outside, if the weather's nice) and clap hands or "dance-walk" while singing the words.

After the active-prayer, it's still not time to impose dead silence and get-down-to-work orders. The lesson itself has to be spiced with activity. Example: if it's Easter time, a miming of the Easter story can be effective, because it will capture the children's attention. Either you or a well-prepared student can read passages from the Easter story at a special desk or podium, while a cast of little "mimers" portrays the event in gestures. Or, if it's Pentecost, better still, because the Pentecost story lends itself easily to activity. The children will have no problem making the sounds for the strong wind in the upper room (without blowing the roof off!). After the wind, the children can portray the coming of the Holy Spirit by holding over their heads big red "flames" on which are printed the gifts and/or fruits of the Holy Spirit. You might list these on the board with a short definition for each.

After that, the children will probably be ready to sit down and discuss the gifts. This can be done by asking, "What gift did you receive? How many in the class received that same gift of the Spirit?" One by one you can discuss the gifts, and what it is that we really receive when we celebrate that gift.

Will learning be occurring? Yes, and the needs of their little bodies will be taken care of while you will be thanking God that re-entry was a little easier this time.

Tips for end-of-year syndrome
During the last days of the school year, it's important to try to stay on schedule—your regular schedule—as much as possible. There's something about a regular schedule that really helps good discipline.

Review needs to done in those last weeks of your faith formation program. But with summer beckoning at every window, it's often difficult to administer written tests to check their knowledge. So, what's to be done? Well, here are a few ideas to begin with:

1) Begin each lesson with prayer that will focus on the need for everyone's cooperation; for example, a prayer that includes both petitions and promises. For example, the first part of the prayer could contain petitions like these:

Jesus, please help us
be as quiet as we can out of courtesy to others,
be helpful,
try to follow directions,
and so on.

The second part could contain promises like these:

Jesus, I promise
to work quietly today,
to try to finish my work on time,
to do what I know is right, for love of you,
and so on.

2) Have several children go to the front of the room or the middle of a circle and pretend that they are senior citizens remembering positive things from the past school year. (You will need to keep them on track.) You could get them started by asking questions such as, "Do you remember the beatitudes project we did at the beginning of the year?" Every once in a while ask the rest of the class whether the "old folks" forgot anything.

3) Have all the items from your table of contents printed on slips of paper. Have a child pick one of the slips and then have the whole class recall all they can about the subject.

Here's something else that can help you get through the end-of-the-year syndrome: do appreciation projects. Many teachers do this by having the children make thank-you cards for the DRE, the pastor, parents, the maintenance staff, and others. You might want to show appreciation in a different way. Place a small branch in a can filled with sand. Give the children strips of paper and have them write down (for the DRE, for the pastor, etc.) "What I like best about you." Tape or glue the strips of papers into rings and hang them on the appropriate branches.

4) Help the children carry their religion lessons through the summer. Remind them how easy it is to forget what they have learned. Have them make posters of what they would especially like to remember when religion classes begin again in the fall. Suggest that they take the posters home and put them in a prominent place.

Another idea is to plan with the children a schedule of daily prayers to say during the summer. You might also want to have them discuss what they can do for family and friends during the summer months.

Let us pray
Jesus, Master Teacher, please give me the wisdom, patience, and skill I need for this first post-vacation (or end-of-the-year) lesson. Help me be sensitive and open to adapting to the children's mood, firm in keeping order, and creative in spicing up work with activity. May I keep your example in front of me. Amen.

For reflection and discussion
- What has been your experience of post-vacation re-entry or end of school year jitters?
- How have you handled situations that arose?
- Share ideas with other catechists about helpful techniques and strategies for end-of-the-year or re-entry lessons.

13

When a Child Won't Cooperate

Who is the "uncooperative child"? If you are an experienced catechist, you will grin at the very question as myriad examples parade through your memory. If you are a beginning teacher, you might wrinkle your brow and wonder a bit.

My experience has been that, just as there are no two "flowers of the field" exactly alike, so no two children are alike. And, I might add, no one catechist will reach out in the same way as another to a child who won't cooperate. Whether we like it or not, each of us brings a unique background in upbringing, education, personality, prejudices, personal quirks, and preconceptions to every class we teach. So each of us will define "uncooperative" in slightly different ways. However, if we were to create a grab bag of what we consider an uncooperative child to be, we might come up with the following:

- A child who regularly comes to class unprepared—no homework, no book—and who has no good excuse for this;

- One who regularly comes late and, of course, doesn't slip quietly into the nearest seat but enters like a performer in a circus (ta-da!), creating complete chaos in the class (to the delight of the other children);

- One who insists, with great and loud arguments, that placing one's name on the bottom of the paper makes a lot more sense than placing it on the top, and in fact, may be more scientifically correct!

- One who challenges every statement you make, not for clarification but to entertain the class and make the time pass more quickly.

These examples are just the tip of the iceberg, but they give you a pretty good idea of what is meant by a child who won't cooperate. No doubt you'll agree that having one or two such children in a class is definitely "water" that cries out to be changed into "wine." The question is: how can this be done?

Being a good catechist, you already know what the first solution is: pray! That's right, pray. Call upon the Master Catechist for the help and guidance you need. Pray for yourself that all the gifts of the Holy Spirit necessary for this particular situation be yours. Pray, too, that each child will receive the same gifts. When we pray in this way, we quickly learn that the Holy Spirit will not do our job for us but will help us see the situation more clearly.

More than meets the eye
Basically children are good, and they want to be able to cooperate with catechists and teachers and have a good relationship with them. It has been my experience that no child routinely disrupts a class or annoys a teacher unless something is going wrong in his or her life. We have to be aware of this and consider various options for dealing with it. What might such options be?

An obvious one is to answer the question, "What is the real problem here?" Following are some of the ways we can find out.

1) Ask the child directly (in private of course): "What is the problem?" You may get only limited information that way because often the child has no idea what the problem is—but it's a start.

2) Study the child's responses in the class—both written and oral—carefully. Notice what the child draws or how he or she colors. Often problems surface clearly in these responses.

3) Plan one of your class activities with that child in mind, then observe. For example, give the child a significant part in a mini-skit, then observe his or her actions and reactions.

4) Talk to parents about your concerns and ask for their suggestions.

If you can uncover the problem, great. You can then take positive action to help the child deal with it. But what if you can't identify a problem and the child still acts out? What then?

Keep the children involved

It's important to keep children as fully involved in the lesson as possible. Give them responsibility as your helpers, the idea being that someone grown up enough to be asked to pass out paper and pencils is certainly grown up enough to behave!

Another option that has worked for me is to force myself to overlook the negative behavior when I can, and pay particular attention to the least sign of positive behavior in an uncooperative child. I praise that good behavior immediately. There's a lot of truth to the old adage that a spoonful of sugar is more effective than all the vinegar in the world!

When I was actively teaching, my own attitude always went a long way toward solving the problem of a child who wouldn't cooperate. My first reaction when I discovered that I had such a child in my class was to roll my eyes heavenward and say, "Lord, why me?" or "Deliver me, O Lord!" I long ago realized, however, that the Master Catechist's attention is elsewhere when we pray like that. Eventually I learned to pray quite a different prayer which went something like this: "Wow, Jesus, you really have confidence in me to have sent this child my way so that I may be of some help." This attitude completely changed how I looked at a child. I no longer saw an uncooperative child but rather a child much loved by Jesus.

It is evident, then, that having an uncooperative child in class is not the end of the world. In fact, it's probably a blessing. True, the child will annoy you, bring out the worst in you, mess up your most beautiful plans, slow down your class' progress, make you lose your cool; but that child may also offer you the opportunity to grow in patience, love, and self-control. And, even more important, he or she may give you the chance to lift the burden from their shoulders. It's your opportunity to live the words of Jesus: "Just as you did it to one of the least of these who are members of my family, you did it to me." What else could be as important in your teaching as that?

Let us pray
Master Teacher, you who loved children so much, help me with _____ (name the child). Please give me the gifts and resources I need to lift whatever burden assails this child. Show me the way to go so that both of us, the child and I, may conclude this class closer to you in every way. I ask this in your holy name. Amen.

For reflection and discussion
- How would you describe an "uncooperative child"?
- Terms like "uncooperative child" are used in this book to help describe discipline issues. However, assigning labels like these to children in your class can have a negative impact on the way you perceive and on what you expect from the child. Do you find yourself using these kinds of labels? What can you do to keep from labeling children?
- What techniques/approaches have you used in teaching a child who is often uncooperative?

14

When There's Not Enough Activity

If the children in your class never stop moving, maybe it's because they need more activity, the kind that gives them a break and draws their attention back to your lesson.

Wouldn't it be wonderful if we could adjust the motors of our youngsters to keep them in their seats and quiet for an hour as we lecture away about the beauty of the Good News? The very concept makes us laugh because we know we will have discipline problems if we keep children inactive for too long. In fact, one of the most common causes for discipline problems in religion class is inactivity. Too much sit-down-and-be-quiet! What can you do about this? Well, several things.

First, you need to be aware of the attention span of your particular age group. How do you do this? Usually the information is in your teacher's manual, but if not, you can get it from books on classroom management in the public library. Or ask a Catholic or public school teacher with your same age group for some input.

Second, decide on some appropriate physical activities that

you can do at break points during your sessions or when your youngsters get too "wiggly." If possible ask a physical education teacher for her or his suggestions. Keep a small file box with a variety of short activities in it. The following are several such activities that I have picked up during my years of teaching.

Activity ideas

1) Punch the ceiling. Have the children stand and stretch to the limit, then attempt to punch the ceiling. The little rascals love this activity because, let's face it, young members of the human race like to punch anything! By having them aim at the ceiling, you ensure that they won't accidently punch their nearest neighbor. This simple activity relaxes the children and you, too (for you should be doing the exercises along with them). Such activity also serves to relieve growing muscles, helps the children let off steam and frustration, and takes very little class time.

2) Follow the directions. This activity involves giving the children a series of short directions, such as, "Stand up, place both feet firmly on the floor, reach up to the ceiling with both hands, sit down, fold your hands." When done quickly a few times, this is a great break, and children enjoy the pace.

3) The ladder. For this activity have the children quickly touch (1) head, (2) shoulders, (3) waist, (4) knees, and (5) feet, as they count from one to five. Then reverse the process—feet, knees, waist, shoulders, and head—and count backwards. They only need to do this a couple of times because it takes more energy than it seems at first.

4) Tiptoe in place. You have to be careful with this one, especially if there's a meeting space below yours. The idea is for the children to stand and then pretend to be running on tiptoe but in place—without making noise. If they make too much noise, just say, "Oops! I guess we can't do this one because we'll disturb the other classes." They'll promise to do it quietly, and they usually will.

5) Stand up, sit down. For this activity tell the children you are going to read a paragraph, a poem, or part of a story. Every time you say the word "and," they are to stand up and sit down quickly. Make sure your selection has the "ands" spaced out, so the children won't be trying to stand up and sit down at the same time.

6) Singing with motions. Another way to keep your class alert is to have them sing a lively hymn with lively motions. Good examples of such hymns include: "Every Time I Feel the Spirit," "This Little Light of Mine," "I've Got that Joy, Joy, Joy," and "Soon and Very Soon." (All of these can be found in the hymnal *Lead Me, Guide Me*, GIA Publications.)

If you teach for more than an hour at a time, you might want to take a more substantial break. For example, have the children go outside for a quick run around the playground or somewhere else that's safe (check with your DRE ahead of time). The children will come back full of fresh air and ready to settle down for the rest of the session. Be sure to establish a signal for this so children will know when you want them back. It's also best to set boundaries: "Run to the fence (or the tree or the big rock...) and back."

For additional short activities ask your DRE and other catechists what they do to keep children active and interested. Jot their suggestions down for your activity file. The important thing is that you are conscious of the physical needs of those you teach, and want to keep them involved in your lesson. The children may not realize why they always feel so good when they leave your class (and they will feel good if you keep their attention and give them the right amount of activity). However, you will have the satisfaction and reward of knowing that it's due to your thoughtfulness.

Let us pray

Jesus, you know about the growing pains of children. Please help me to be aware of them, too. Inspire me to make the effort and take the time to address their physical needs. Fill my heart with your own love for them. Amen.

For reflection and discussion

- How much physical activity do you include in your lesson plan (including moving from individual work to group work, standing and stretching, etc.)?

- What "activity breaks" have worked well for you? Share experiences with other catechists and start (or add to) your own file of ideas for short activities.

15

When Children Fall Behind

Sometimes a child or two will be behind the others as far as religious knowledge is concerned. (Sometimes it's the whole class.) Perhaps they were sick for a time, or had to drop out because of family problems, or are newly arrived in the area. Whatever the reason, children can and will fall behind the others in their class. But there are definite things you can do to help them catch up. To determine just how far behind these youngsters might be, try the following game (it's also a good review for your whole class).

Going to the store
On index cards write the titles of the prayers your class should know and questions about the general information your class is studying. Have children move into a circle, and give each child (and yourself) one of the cards.

Now, let's say that your card says, "Our Father." Explain that this game is called "Store," because you are going to pretend to go to the store to get information. Walk inside the circle and stop in front of one child. Ask, "Do you have this in your store?" Show the card. The child then gives you what you ask for by saying the Our Father. (Note: if the child doesn't know the answer, he or she tells you at which "store" you can get it. That way, no one is embarrassed.) The next person shows a card that might say, "What is a sacrament?" The child whose "store" is being visited fills the order by giving the definition of a sacrament.

Continue until all the cards are used and you have recorded the responses. If your new students (or others) keep passing their turn, make note of the items they didn't know. Later they can be helped by individual instruction from you and your helpers.

A prayer review
Besides having new children who are behind, it sometimes happens that a whole class may be behind. What to do then? Perhaps you need to check whether the children know the prayers they learned at previous levels. Usually the prayers are repeated at each age level. Have the children cut out a simple figure (a paper-doll, cat, dog—whatever). Have them tape the figure to a pencil, a twig, or a popsicle stick. For fun, they can name the figure.

Then, list on the board the prayers the children should know. Have them give their figure a check up on the prayers. On a sheet of paper or on a card, the children can list the prayers the figure knows without looking at the book. If some of the prayers are missing (meaning that the child doesn't know those particular prayers), the child can "tutor" the figure until the prayers are memorized.

After this activity have the children write their names on the lists and give them to you. You will have the information you need without having humiliated anyone, without having criticized previous catechists, and without having created any significant discipline problems, because the activity is fun. You can go from there to teach what you need to teach.

Filling in the blanks

At times you may discover that the groundwork for the material you have to teach has not been done by previous catechists. Here's one way to provide this kind of missing information. Make a game out of it. Have your group form a circle, and tell them you are going to be their secretary. Have the children tell you all they can remember about your subject for the day, and write it down. Then list the answers on the board, on a large sheet of newsprint, or on a sheet of paper on your desk. Suggest a few items of your own and you will be slowly helping your class to catch up.

This kind of catching up might take several sessions, but it can be done quickly and will not set you back too much. Believe me, it's worth it! One very wise DRE has her catechists check their scope-and-sequence charts at the end of the year and list which items they were unable to cover. (That DRE had established such a comfortable climate for her volunteers that they didn't feel threatened by this.)

Having a few children or even a whole class fall behind is no disaster. As you can see, the situation can be remedied with a little good will and a whole lot of help from the Master Teacher. After all, the most important thing is that the children are growing in their love for and relationship with Christ.

Pass-the-question review relay

In a small box place slips of paper on which you've written questions relating to the material you're reviewing. (You'll need at least one slip for each child, plus a few more.) Make a hole in the cover of the box, big enough for a child's hand. Pass the box down one row. The first child takes a slip, reads the question, gives the answer, keeps the slip, and passes the box on to the next child. (This procedure is followed whether the child's answer is right or wrong.) At the end of the relay, the children who have missed each try their own question again with "helpful hints" from the rest of the class, or they try a new question. The goal here is review and cooperative learning, not competition.

Let us pray

Jesus, so often you took negative situations and turned them around. Please show us how to help our children through periods when they fall behind. Help us to be gentle and patient. We ask this in your name. Amen.

For reflection and discussion

- Have you determined whether any of the children in your class are behind in their religious studies?

- What steps have you taken to help them catch up?

- Besides review activities, what are some options for helping a child who has fallen behind in religious studies, or who has learning difficulties?

16

When You Are Missing Supplies

When you plan a great activity but don't have the supplies to carry it out, what should you do? What can you do?

"I have thirteen children in my group, but only twelve pairs of scissors. You wouldn't have another pair, would you?" Your good DRE does a quick search for you but... "Sorry," she says, "not a pair in sight. And wouldn't you know, I just lent mine to the volunteers working on a project downstairs."

On your way back to class you think, "Jesus, you changed water into wine once. Would you please find me one more pair of scissors?" Miracles do happen, and it could be that when you recount your scissors...lo and behold! You find you had miscounted the first time. A more likely scenario, however, is that you will have to make do. As you well know catechists are experts at that. Here are some suggestions.

Alternate ways to go

In the case of the missing pair of scissors, you can pair two of your best-behaved youngsters with one pair of scissors.

Explain that you have confidence that they are mature enough to know how to share the scissors and still get the project done. However, if you are missing several pairs of scissors, you might either adapt the project so you don't need scissors or, better yet, teach the children the art of "tearing" the areas that need cutting.

Let's say, for example, that you've planned an Easter project that necessitates cutting a cross out of pastel-colored paper and gluing it to a white background. Have the children draw the cross, then show them how to gently tear around it. You might even want to use this technique when you have scissors.

Another obstacle

Now you have the crosses all ready, you've given out the white sheets for the background, and it's time to glue. You have a child give out the glue, and by now you feel pretty happy about the project. But what's this...one child after another complains that the glue is hard as a rock! Sure enough, somehow all the glue has dried out. What's to be done?

Suddenly you remember your plastic container of flour. (Note: experienced catechists know that you always have your container of flour ready for emergencies!) You take out your container and mix flour with water until it has the consistency of drop cookies. Taking a popsicle stick (another regular item in your supply box) you put a glob of your flour mixture on a piece of paper for each child, and you're ready to finish the project!

After you give thanks to Jesus, you have a right to feel good. After all, look what you've done! You didn't lose your cool. You didn't run off. You found a way to finish your project. And, perhaps most important of all, you taught the children that they don't have to have the best of everything to do a good job! You've taught them to economize, to make do, and you've given them an example of how to handle a frustrating situation.

Where to get resources

There are other sources of help when you are short on materials you need to do a good job: the children in your class and their families and friends, for starters. Do you need boxes? One family has someone working at the supermarket. No problem. You can get all the boxes you need. Do you need all kinds of pictures? No problem. One of your children's parents works in a card shop where cards and envelopes are discarded regularly. You can get them for the asking.

Yard or garage sales, thrift shops, school bazaars, and lumber yards are other possible sources for materials. I have also found that religious good merchants are often willing to donate end-of-the-line religious articles, holy pictures, posters, and so on.

Ask the parish, too

You might want to encourage your DRE to make a list of supplies needed for your catechetical program and publish the list in the parish bulletin or as an insert. Not only would that help the program but it would involve more people in the program, a real advantage to all concerned.

Last but not least, God has provided us with a whole outdoors full of supplies for our sessions: twigs to hang banners on, flowers for prayer corners, rocks to decorate, leaves to use as patterns for prayer bookmarks, and more.

So in the future, when you find you are lacking some material to complete a project, see it as a chance to employ the wonderful gifts of creativity God has given you. "The Lord will guide you continually, and satisfy your needs..." (Isaiah 58:11).

> **Let us pray**
>
> Jesus, model of catechists, you did a wonderful job of teaching, without a lot of fancy equipment. Your "classroom" was wherever you found yourself at the moment: a hillside, a small boat, a

portico of a temple, a roadside. Your audiovisuals were the lilies of the field and the birds of the air, tiny seeds and big storms, a little child and a widow slipping her last coin into the collection box.

Please help me to make do, to be creative in using what is available, and not always to demand only the best for my religion class and projects. Help me, Jesus, to find joy in teaching a *big* message with small resources when that's necessary.

Above all, Jesus, help me to have and to help my youngsters have the conviction that God will always provide for us because we are those precious little sparrows God keeps an eye on! Amen.

For reflection and discussion

- Reread some of your favorite gospel parables in which Jesus uses concrete objects/images to communicate a message (e.g., the sower and the seed: Matthew 13; birds of the air and lilies of the field: Matthew 6:25–33; the ten bridesmaids: Matthew 25:1–13; the lost sheep: Luke 15:3–7; the prodigal son: Luke 15:11–32). How can you employ the same technique in your religion class?

- The lack of supplies may sometimes be solved by more thorough preparation. When you prepare your lesson plan, do you make a list of the materials you need and check ahead of time to see whether they're available?

- Make a file of games and other activities that require a bare minimum of materials.

17

When There's Not Enough Time

What do you do when the clock is winding down and you are just gearing up?

Is there anything more frustrating for a catechist than to have a head full of ideas, an armful of projects, a heart full of zeal and enthusiasm, and suddenly, no time left? Well, it happens all the time. When a happy, dedicated teacher is intent on sharing the Good News with a roomful of children, that old clock gets to spinning around at top speed. That's just the way it is.

At such times we might be tempted to think: wouldn't it be great if we, like Jesus, had the luxury of sitting on a slab of rock on the side of a hill, with all the time in the world to get our message across? But Jesus had time limits, as well as distracted and fidgety listeners, unbelieving listeners, skeptics, and so on, to deal with. It's the same for us. And no matter how things seem, Jesus can and does help us make the most of the time we have to do our ministry well.

Let's look at some time-saving devices and procedures that

can give you the maximum time for teaching the essentials of the faith. I think the best way to do this is to "walk through" a typical class (if such a thing exists!) and see how you might save time at the various stages.

Being organized

The first and most important timesaver for any catechist is good organization. You need to know ahead of time what materials you are going to use; you need to have these ready; you need a set of procedures for passing things out; and you need to know how you will handle latecomers and others who might potentially disrupt your class. Keep in mind that nothing eats up class time like ahems! You know: "Ahem...let's see now, how are we going to do this?" or "Ahem...should we do this now or wait until next time?" By the time you finish your ahems, the children are ready with theirs, and the session is a disaster.

Getting there early

The second thing you need to do is arrange your time so that you arrive early enough to set up before the children come. To do this, determine how much time you require for preparation. Some classes, as we all know, call for more time to set up than others. Although there will be times when emergencies arise and pre-class set-up is impossible, you will still want to aim at the ideal. When children come into class and see that you are ready for them, they pick up the message, "This class is important!"

Starting on time

Another timesaver is to begin class right away. There are always some children who show up with something to distract you and the other children, hoping to delay the start of class as long as possible. For example, a child may enter class with a segment of creation that hops, crawls, squeaks, or (saints preserve us!) slithers. What's to be done? First, say a fast (very fast) prayer like, "Jesus, please. Don't let me pass out!" then ask the youngster to put the crawly-creepy treasure in a safe place, well secured against escape, until the end of class when there may be time to view it.

Another reason we often lose precious class time is that we have to deal with late arrivals (a continuing problem in parish religious education settings). Prepare for this eventuality ahead of time by giving clear instructions about what children should do if they arrive late. Instruct them to come in quietly and to sit in a designated place until you reach a break point in the lesson. Then and only then can they move closer and join the group.

Be sure not to blame or embarrass children who arrive late; they are often being dropped off by a parent who is running late. However, you do need to clearly explain how important it is not to interrupt a class in progress. You can't imagine how much time you will gain with this proviso in place.

Don't do all the talking

Learning to restrict your words is another way to use time well. At times you'll need to practice this skill outside of class. In my early teaching days I had the idea that my words were pearls of wisdom that my students would receive eagerly and with awe. Well, it took only a few sessions of spit-ball tossing, yawning and stretching, and an endless parade of youngsters going to the restroom to instill in me a deep humility that hadn't been there before. It isn't easy to say to yourself, "Be quiet!"—but I learned.

A good adage might be: "Blessed be the teacher who does not use two words to give directions when one word will do." These days, when children are bombarded with words day and night, you might as well conserve your energy because they won't listen to your long declarations anyway. Instead, give them several ways to respond to your words of wisdom. Have them look in their Bibles for passages that relate to your lesson. Have them prepare petitions or prayers of thanksgiving based on the lesson content. Invite them to occasionally teach an aspect of the lesson, and so on. Once you start thinking of ways to talk less and have children do more, you'll have more interesting lessons as well.

More timesavers

Besides the above four essential timesavers here are two more:

Delegate. Let the children do some of the organizational jobs. Train them on the proper way to take attendance, erase boards, give out materials, move tables and chairs, and prepare equipment in an orderly and efficient manner. Depending on their age level, children can take care of windows, doors, maps and charts, supplies, clean up, and all kinds of things that will save you time.

Solve problems quickly, whenever possible. You can take care of discipline problems without long speeches and due process. You can show compassion without giving excessive attention to one child. You get the idea.

After trying some of these timesaving devices, you'll develop others that are even better suited to your own unique teaching situation.

Let us pray

Time is your creation, blessed God, and you have given into my hands all the time I need to do a good job with this class. I ask for your help and grace to use this gift of time in such a way that all of us may be drawn closer to you, and that your holy plan may be fulfilled in us. Amen.

For reflection and discussion

- Think about a few of your recent sessions. How well did you use the time you had? Did you spend too much time getting the lesson started? Did disruptions continue for too long? Discuss with other catechists what you can do to remedy the situation.

- What tasks can you delegate to save time in organizing materials and activities?

- Study your presentations. Are they too wordy? Do you spend a lot of time talking? How can you make your lessons more concise and to the point, yet fun?

18

When Children Are Falling Asleep

Though you can't always control the physical environment in your class, you can be sensitive to children's needs. In this chapter we'll take a look at some positive ways to meet the physical needs of those you teach (and thus greatly reduce discipline problems). These include: lighting, ventilation, hunger, seating arrangements, and physical and mental fatigue. On the face of it, these do not seem related to discipline, but indeed they are, as we will see.

Poor lighting

A child who has to struggle with improper lighting for an hour or so will act up. So would we! Signs that indicate poor lighting are: squinting when reading a book or paper; sitting sideways in a desk; or rubbing their eyes. We need to develop a keen sense of observation to be aware of these behaviors. Once noticed, what can you do?

First, try moving the child to another area or turning the child's seat to face another angle, or, if the "climate" in your room allows this, have the child find his/her own proper lighting space. If the problem is that lighting is poor everywhere in the room, try to keep the children alert by going outside (when possible) for part of your lessons.

Poor ventilation

Have you ever entered a classroom and been nearly overcome with the heavy, stale air? Children's reactions to this kind of room will be sleepiness or fidgeting. In both cases they will likely be unaware of the source of their discomfort.

In good weather or in warmer climates it's easy to provide adequate ventilation: just open the windows. But if it's ten-degrees below zero or ninety-degrees above zero outdoors, how do we provide sufficient fresh air? When you notice that the children are drifting off or getting restless, you might want to do what I call the fresh-air exercise. Here's how it goes.

Assign the various windows in your meeting space to specific children, who will open them when you say, "Come in, fresh air!" When the windows are open, and the cold air begins to spread through the room, say, "Welcome, fresh air!" That's the signal for the children to stand, face the windows, and inhale-exhale for a minute or so—however, not long enough for the children to actually get cold!

Will some youngsters overdo the inhale-exhale exercise? Of course! Just expect it! Then say, "Thank you, God, for fresh air!" and have the children repeat it. That's the signal for the children to sit down and for the "window-monitors" to close the windows. This exercise clears your room of stale air—at least temporarily—and drives the cobwebs out of heads!

If children are hungry

When children attend religion class immediately after school, they often arrive hungry. The first and best solution is to bring an easy-to-eat snack to class: graham crackers, fruit sticks, oyster crackers (no candy or junk foods). A couple of graham crackers served on a small napkin are not messy and can be eaten a little at a time during the session. Feeding hungry children may not be in our teacher's manual, but it was on the agenda of the Master Teacher when he saw that people were hungry (see Matthew 15:32–39). (Of course, you'll want to check with your DRE before giving the youngsters anything to eat.)

Seating arrangements

To achieve a good learning climate and good discipline as well, a teacher needs to be aware of the value of appropriate seating. This seems so simple, yet seating can make the difference between a class that runs smoothly and one that is plagued with discipline crises.

Desks or seats in rows are still good for some things, but the most child-friendly seating arrangements are the most effective. For example:

- seating in small groups for discussion and/or group study, drill, or group projects;

- sitting in a large circle for total-group discussion, circle learning games, role-playing, or problem-solving situations;

- sitting on the floor for some projects involving large posters or equipment.

Sometimes you may have to keep an eye on a jittery child who may need to sit closer to you and/or near the front of your teaching space. And remember that distractible children need seating that is protected from other visual-auditory stimuli.

Mental or physical fatigue

A child who is tired—mentally or physically—will do one of two things: act up or go to sleep. In either case we won't be able to teach the child. If the fatigue is mental, the child will complain that the work is "too hard" or "boring." Be able to adapt a little when necessary. Have the children do most of the task, then allow them to take a brief rest. You can say,

"I've noticed you seem a bit sleepy, so let's take a break." "Taking a break" means the children can put their heads down on the desk (or table) for a minute or so. Note: again this usually occurs when religion classes are right after school.

When you do all you can in each of these areas, you are a thoughtful catechist indeed. Being thoughtful of children never sets a teacher back—never! On the contrary, we teach best when we teach as Jesus taught, with compassion and love.

Let us pray

Jesus, thank you for the help you give us in this area of discipline. Please help us apply what we've learned about good discipline in every session we ever teach. May we always remember that when we treat others—especially our children—with compassion and love, we show love and compassion to you. Amen.

For reflection and discussion

- Evaluate the physical environment of your meeting space: lighting, ventilation, seating arrangements, visuals. Do any of them need improvement? What might you do to improve these elements?

- Does your group meet at the end of a school day? What techniques or activities have you used successfully to teach children who are tired after a full day of school?

- Make a list of your ideas and share/swap them with other catechists.

19

When You're Not Prepared

One of the first rules for good discipline is good preparation. If you enter religion class without a clue as to what you are doing, the children will give you plenty to do just keeping them from causing mayhem.

Going into class unprepared should happen only in rare, emergency circumstances. If such an emergency does occur, however, here are some pointers that might help

Enlist the children's help

First, apologize to the children for coming to them unprepared and explain the reason for the situation. (Children are wonderful. Most of the time they'll take you under their wing and do their best to try to help you.) Gather them around you and ask them to pray over you, asking Jesus to give you the skill and wisdom needed to give them a good class and to help them help you. This simple action will take care of many discipline problems because it puts everyone in a shared-responsibility mode.

After the prayer quickly find the lesson that comes next in sequence in your text, and present it the best way you can. You might read the lesson with the children or have them read it. At the end of class enlist the children's help again by inviting them to say spontaneous prayers. Finish by thanking God for a good class.

Instant activities

Although you haven't prepared any activities to go with the day's lesson, all you need are a few techniques and materials. You should always have "standby materials" on hand: paper, pencils, charts, crayons, etc.

Quickly choose one or two "instant activities" from your activity box (if you don't have one, see below). Adapt the activities to the content of the day's lesson. For example, if your subject is the fourth commandment, you might have the children role-play related situations, or you could ask them to make up prayers for their parents, grandparents, or guardians.

One instant activity that generally works well is to give out paper and invite the children to do a "comic strip" mural on the board or wall or a large piece of cardboard. For example, if your lesson is about one of Jesus' parables, make a list of the sequence of events in that parable and number them, then assign the drawings. When the drawings are finished, put them on the board in sequence. You can then teach or review the parable using the drawings, and discuss with the children its application to their lives.

With God's help you can avoid a discipline crisis when you have to go to class unprepared. It's just a matter of making use of the instant helps available to you.

How to make an Activity Box

1) Get a file or file folder and index cards.
2) Write on the index cards any activity ideas you find in books, magazines, and elsewhere.
3) Design a filing system that works for you.

Let us pray

Jesus, beloved Teacher, help us remember that you are always with us, enabling us to handle with love the challenges of our ministry. May we lead our children to you by sharing with them your Good News. Amen.

For reflection and discussion

- What are some reasons/situations that might cause you to come to class unprepared? Which of these are truly unavoidable? What might you do ahead of time to forestall or offset these situations?

- Another alternative for the days when you are unprepared: keep a few stock lesson plans on hand for such emergencies. Write down two or three ideas for themes/subjects appropriate for the grade level of your youngsters and the for the program of that grade. Develop a simple but complete lesson plan for each of these subjects, and keep them on file.

- Storytelling is another approach. If the lesson is on forgiveness, for example, tell the story of the prodigal son with lots of expression, and invite the children to act it out. Then discuss how each of the persons in the story felt and what they experienced.

20

When You Need Another Approach

You planned your lesson well. You developed review tactics and projects and designed clever worksheets. You read up on your material, and you made notes from the Bible, the *Catechism of the Catholic Church,* and other sources. Once the session started, you made sure the children were comfortably seated and that there was plenty of fresh air in the room. You made your meeting space as attractive as you could. Yet, after all this the children's reaction is, "Duh!" What can you do to "turn around" a situation like this?

We need God

If you believe that everything you do as a catechist depends on you, then you might believe such a situation is hopeless. But if you spend quality time with Jesus regularly, it will be easy to remind yourself, "Hey! I don't have to see results to know that God's work will be done in this class. All I am expected to do is do the best I can. God will take it from there, no matter how things look!" Suddenly, in spite of yourself, you'll begin to feel better, knowing that those precious young Christians you're working with don't have to be dancing to your tune in order for God's grace to be operating in them.

A short prayer will help, too. "Jesus, I've done the best I can. Please take it from there, okay?" That prayer is similar to Mary's prayer at Cana: "Jesus, they have no wine!" Knowing that the end result doesn't depend on you allows you to be at peace, knowing as Mary did that the water of seeing no results will be turned into wine by God's action.

That will take care of your attitude, but what are you going to do about the lesson?

You need to adjust

It's always disappointing when your plan isn't working, but sometimes you just have to acknowledge that the soil of this class is not ready for the seed of this particular preparation. You'll have to try another approach. So, you put aside your original plan and adjust to the movement of the Spirit. (Don't grieve over your original plan; you'll be able to use it later.)

Here's one example of adjusting to the Spirit. Let's say your lesson is about forgiveness. You can ask yourself: "What do these children like to do best? How can I still communicate the substance of this lesson?"

You know that your children really enjoy role-playing, so you suggest several situations that call for forgiveness. You invite the youngsters to take turns role-playing these situations. You might then ask them to role-play scenes from the gospel that illustrate forgiveness, for example, the story of the prodigal son (Luke 15:11–32) or the woman who washed Jesus' feet with perfume (Matthew 26:6–13). Invite the children to offer spontaneous prayers ˍasking God's forgiveness for themselves, their families, their country, and the world. Also allow two or three minutes for silent prayer so the children can talk to Jesus about their personal need for forgiveness.

You won't believe how sweet the "turnaround" will be at the end of that session. Because you were willing to sacrifice your original plan and adapt to the situation of your youngsters, you will all leave the session with lighter hearts, and perhaps with new insights into your lesson as well.

Try to be flexible

Having to completely change your approach is not likely to happen often, but it does happen. So it's important to have alternate activities available at short notice. I recommend keeping a small file with 3" x 5" index cards filled with such activities. Each time you plan a lesson, select several alternate activities to take along—just in case! Put a notation in your lesson plan to remind you they're there. If you need one, use it.

The next time you see that your pearls of wisdom have no takers, don't be upset. Just hold on to your content but change your strategy. It's as simple as that!

Let us pray

Jesus, on some days your listeners weren't "with you," either. They didn't understand, and nothing happened in those "classes" of yours...or did it? What did you do? You kept the content of your message but changed your strategy, adapting to your listeners.

Please help me be humble enough to put my lesson plans aside when necessary, and flexible enough to adapt my message—which is your message—to the precious children I teach. Amen.

For reflection and discussion

- Reflect on your teaching style. Do you feel comfortable thinking "on your feet," that is, being spontaneous? Or do you feel the need to be structured, relying heavily on your lesson plan? If you tend to be spontaneous, then you probably won't have a problem adapting a lesson. But if you need more organization, you may want to build an alternate approach to each lesson into your lesson planning. Some teacher's manuals offer alternate activities for each lesson. If not, create your own.

- Do you find yourself having to change your approach fairly often? If so, you might want to keep a record of what works and what doesn't. Ask yourself why a particular approach doesn't work well with your youngsters. For example, perhaps you are lecturing for too long. Or perhaps you need more physical activity. Perhaps your youngsters need more visuals.

21

When You Feel Overwhelmed

You walk into religion class lugging your lesson plans, your charts, your posters, your video tape, crayons, pencils,...the whole bit. You are supremely prepared—for a change! You are full of pep and singing alleluia in your heart because you anticipate a "gold star" class today.

Knock! Knock! Knock! Your DRE comes to ask if you could possibly take on the other first grade class. The catechist is sick and can't make it, and your DRE has an appointment that can't be cancelled.

"Oh, sure, sure," you respond as you wonder if your material can be adapted to a double-size group. You start to feel overwhelmed as the other first graders come marching through the door.

As if that weren't enough, you are just about to begin your opening prayer when a commotion erupts near the windows: "Mrs. _____! A wasp just flew in!" You're mortally afraid of wasps and you eye the exit, your first impulse being to flee. Instead, you take a deep breath, arm yourself with a fly swatter (or something like it), and take care of that problem!

By the time you have everyone settled down again, fifteen minutes of your precious hour is gone. This sort of situation can happen any time. How can you make a "quick recovery"?

First send an SOS to the Master Catechist: "Jesus, help me...please!" After that, quickly adapt what you can from your lesson. Even with twice the number of children, you can use the prayer service you had planned, but what about the rest of the session?

Pair off

If you had an activity planned that involved handouts and you don't have enough to go around, have the children work in pairs. Or ask the children to draw pictures of favorite things they've learned so far this year, then invite them to share. This is a good way for both groups to review. You could ask them to discuss what they plan to do that week to make Jesus better known.

Games are always a good resource with a large group, especially for review. For example, have one child say the first line of a prayer and the whole class repeat it. The next child says the second line, and the whole class repeats the first and second lines, and so on.

How to make bookmarks

Another fun activity is to have children make bookmarks as a memento of the lesson. You can make a bookmark very quickly. Cut construction paper (varied colors) into one inch strips. Pull out your supply box and cut out pictures of Jesus, Mary, the saints, nature scenes. Let each of the children choose a piece of paper and a picture and glue the picture onto the top of the strip. They can even write a simple thought or prayer on their bookmarks.

Finish with hoopla

When you have a larger than usual group, it's always good to finish up with some kind of hoopla that will make the session memorable, maybe a cheer that the children themselves compose, based on your lesson.

You might want to close this class with the following prayer:

Leader   Thank you, Jesus, that we were able to share this lesson with each other today.

All   (to the tune of "Happy Birthday"):

We thank you, we do.
We thank you, we do.
We thank you, dear Jesus.
We thank you, we do.

Leader   Thank you, Jesus, for being with us during this class.

All   Sing: *We thank you, we do...*
(Continue with rest of song...).

Leader   Thank you, Jesus, for...(here invite children to offer prayers).

All   Sing: *We thank you, we do...*
(Continue with rest of song...).

As you can see, if you are prepared to involve children, keep them active, and give them ways to cooperate, any religion session can be a success, in spite of surprises or setbacks.

Let us pray

Jesus, so often in your life too much happened all at once! What did you do? You prayed, then rolled up your sleeves and set about making the best of the situation. In my work as a catechist, when too many things come at me, teach me first of all to call on you. Then, like you, show me how to roll up my sleeves and set about making the best of the situation. Amen.

For reflection and discussion

- Do you have some "quick aids" you use when you're feeling overwhelmed? (e.g., breathing deeply, replacing negative thoughts with positive ones, etc.) ?

- Picture a few scenarios in religion class where things happen that would make you feel overwhelmed (not everyone is overwhelmed by the same things). Ask yourself how you might handle those situations.

- Do you pray for wisdom? Do you try to keep things in perspective? Do you see obstacles as potential opportunities? Share your ideas and fears with other catechists with whom you feel comfortable.

22

When You Need the Right Words

When it comes to children, the clearer we are the better.

Poor discipline can sometimes be caused by our own inability to communicate. Perhaps we are not using appropriate vocabulary for the children, or not using age-appropriate activities and materials. Or, we may not be adapting to "the times." Here are some guidelines to assist you in these three areas.

The words we use

A volunteer catechist who has recently retired from teaching at the university level would probably find it difficult—if not impossible—to speak "God language" to first graders. I once knew such a catechist. When one of her first graders wailed, "I lost my penny," the catechist replied (with much compassion), "Poor dear! I'm certainly distressed over your financial difficulty." That reply shocked the child into forgetting all about the penny!

As always, prayer for God's help should be first on our list of solutions. After praying we can try the following.

- Get a "feel" for age-appropriate vocabulary for the youngsters you are teaching by borrowing a reader, speller, and/or teacher's manual from a local school. Immerse yourself in the vocabulary lists (usually found in the back of these books).

- Go to the children's section in your public library and find age-appropriate books. Spend time reading these to become acquainted with the vocabulary used. If in doubt about which books are age-appropriate, ask the children's librarian for suggestions. He or she will no doubt provide you with just the right books, and even videos and computer materials.

- You might try watching children's cartoons on TV. This is an excellent way to find out what children are able to comprehend. If you are into computers, visit a children's web site and look for information there.

Even with all these helps, you might occasionally slip and say, "God is omnipotent!" instead of "God can do all things." But that's okay. You're only human.

Age-appropriate materials

In order to be an effective instrument in God's hands and maintain good discipline, it's also important to use age-appropriate materials.

We know that eye-hand coordination and audio, visual, and kinesthetic skills develop gradually in human beings. In order to achieve a good learning climate, the catechist needs to adapt materials to the age and learning styles of children.

Following are some ways you can do this.

- When making charts and teaching materials, don't use an overwhelming amount of information. Have fewer items on your charts, posters, and printed materials; and make sure the designs are large and colorful. This makes it easier for young eyes that aren't fully developed yet to take in the material. I might add here that it's important not to give older children materials that are below them. They might interpret this as an insult to their maturity.

- It's well to remember that children's attention spans are very short (and the younger the child, the shorter the span). Just try playing a tape in which the "talking" goes on for more than three minutes! Or try to lecture for that length of time. You simply lose children, and when this happens you can expect discipline problems.

So, what can you do? If you need to use a tape, it's essential to accompany it with colorful charts, flash cards, or pictures, so that both audio and visual skills are engaged. The same is true when you are presenting the material orally, lecture-style (which we sometimes do even though we realize this is not the most effective means of communicating the message to primary-age children). But when an oral presentation is necessary, talk a little, show a picture, talk a little more, ask a question, and so on. Children cannot sit still and listen for long, no matter how hard they try. If we insist they do, then they will insist we accept the consequences: discipline problems.

Adapting to the times

If you're trying to teach something about the family, and the only picture you have on hand is a family from the 1960s, don't use it. Kids will turn it off or get caught up in the "funny" hairstyles. You can easily find contemporary pictures in current magazines. Keep in mind, too, that your children come from all different types of households: single parent homes, parents who've divorced and remarried, foster homes, homes where they live with grandparents or other relatives.

You also need to watch your use of idioms. For example, years ago the expression "a bunch of malarkey" was commonly understood, but today's children might ask, "What's a malarkey?" Try explaining that! How do we adapt our use of idioms to the times? Listen to the children when they are talking to their friends; read their magazines and comic books; watch their TV shows.

Adapting to the times also means keeping updated in the field of catechesis, in methodology, content, means of presentation, and so on. Your DRE will assist you in this area, and your parish library will have books you can consult.

When you have discipline problems, take advantage of the resources and advice available to you in the experience of others, in the materials at your disposal, and above all in God's constant help. All you need do is ask.

Let us pray

Jesus, you said, "Come to me all you who are burdened, and I will give you rest." I sometimes feel very "burdened" with discipline problems, and I need your help. May I see each child I teach as a unique and wonderful person who is dearly loved by you. Help me to love each one as you do, and to find a way to keep young hearts and minds focused on you and your holy Word. Amen.

For reflection and discussion

- Evaluate the vocabulary you use with your youngsters. Is it age appropriate? Are you up-to-date in catechetical content and means of presentation? If not, what steps can you take to update yourself?

- Do you accompany your words with visuals as much as possible (pictures, maps, charts, etc.)?

- Watch one or two TV shows that target your children's age group. Take notes on the language, themes, relationships, etc. Discuss your findings with other catechists.

23

When You Send Mixed Messages

Sometimes discipline problems can be solved simply by making good use of body language, voice, and eyes. Let's look at a few ways this can be done.

It is a fact that imprecise body language confuses children and can lead to discipline problems. For example, if we proclaim the joy of the Lord with our voices but actually have drooping shoulders, limp arms, and a generally unhappy appearance, the children may rightly wonder: "What is the truth here?" The wonderful message we mean to communicate is lost.

Perhaps we are just too tired or sad to do a joy-act with our bodies on any given day. Well, we have options. We can skip talking about joy that day; or we can ask Jesus for help, put our personal problems aside for one hour, square our shoulders, stand up tall, smile, and welcome our youngsters into the miracle of this gift of God called joy.

Another element of body language that can lead to discipline problems is use of jittery motions which indicate that we're really not sure what to do first or what direction to take. This kind of body language gives the impression of disorder. Children will fill the vacuum in no time with body language of their own.

The same can be said for body language such as nervously picking things up and putting them down (indicating indecisiveness) and traveling all over the room for no reason. This kind of body language is unprofessional and distracting. If we have discipline problems, we should observe whether we show this kind of behavior.

What can I do?

If you think you have a problem with distracting body language, there are steps you can take to correct it. First of all, become aware of whether or not you do any of the things I've mentioned, then work to eliminate them. You might ask your DRE or another catechist with whom you feel comfortable to observe some of your classes and let you know if you display negative body language. Also, watch the youngsters in your class. Believe me, there is no better mirror in the whole wide world than a class full of children.

For example, if you display peculiar body language, they'll entertain one another by mimicking you. If you are disorganized and off the track, they'll reflect that. If, instead, you are calm, well-organized, and well-prepared, the children will tend to be calmer and more attentive.

What about your voice?

Sometimes "negative" use of your voice can cause discipline problems. This might not be immediately apparent, but experience proves that it's so. A teacher's poor use of voice can sometimes even be an impediment to learning. For example, suppose a catechist has a tendency to drone while speaking. You know the sound: a voice that stays in the same tone, neither up nor down. A person with a droning voice might say: "Sorry! That's the way God made me! I have a drony voice, and there's nothing I can do about it!" Not true.

Here's something you can do. Take a book—any book—and record yourself reading a paragraph. When you listen to the tape, your reaction may be, "Yuk!"

Now take the same paragraph and read it naturally, as though you were speaking it. Mark the words on which your voice goes up (^) or down (`) naturally. Then record the passage again, inflecting your voice according to the marks you made (you may need to practice a few times first). You will probably be surprised at the difference.

Next underline the words in the paragraph that need to be emphasized. Record the paragraph again with the inflection and the emphasis. This time you won't believe that voice belongs to you!

Too much talking

Another voice-related behavior that can lead to discipline problems might be called "word flooding." What I am referring to is talking too much and for too long a time. Obviously when you teach you have to talk, but it doesn't have to be nonstop, does it? The best cure for this teaching "disability" is good preparation. When we know our subject and our youngsters, we don't have to go on and on.

A conversational type of teaching can help us avoid the "word flooding" problem. For example, teach a little, then ask questions, ask for opinions or responses, challenge and encourage reactions, then repeat the process.

Another aid to good discipline is knowing when to use your "you must do this" voice and when to use your "would you like to do this?" voice. The first goes with tasks and behaviors that are not optional. The second is used with tasks and behaviors that involve children's choices.

Try whispering

When things get out of hand in religion class, you can use the "whisper" or "silence" method. If the class is already loud, what good does it do to add to the noise? Instead, just begin whispering, or keep silent altogether and wait. Watch the effect! Things will definitely tone down.

Several other ways to use our voices in spreading the Good News include putting a smile in our voices, and using correct English, i.e., not slang or kid-talk.

Here's a final suggestion that you can offer to your DRE. When he or she is looking for ideas for your one-day workshops or professional talks, why not invite a local speech therapist? You might be able to find a volunteer in your own parish by placing a request in the Sunday bulletin. A speech therapist would be able to show your whole staff how to use your voices to further the kingdom.

The eyes have it

Eyes can be powerful aids in achieving good discipline in religion class. Here are a few ideas on how it's done.

One way is what I call "the sweep." Instead of concentrating your glance on just a small portion of your class or on an individual child, you can let your eyes "sweep" over the whole group. That tends to make everyone feel involved and encourages good attention. Of course, you will still want to maintain eye contact with each child as the lesson progresses.

Another way might be to deliberately "soften" the look in your eyes when looking directly at a child. When I was taught that skill, I was encouraged to practice on a field of daisies in the country. Or, if I couldn't get to the country, I pretended to be there. (It's actually quite relaxing to do this.) Using a mirror to practice "eye-softening" can also be a help. You may think there's no value in this; you may even think it's nonsense, but it isn't! I've found that when a child (or anyone, for that matter) meets soft, friendly, smiling eyes, he or she is more comfortable and an effective line of communication is open. This is especially important when setting down a few rules of discipline.

For example, if you want the children to return to task after an interruption, you might say, "Time to get back to work now." The result will be much more effective if said with "soft" eyes than if you have a "I dare you to disobey me" look in your eyes.

You see, with a little effort you can use body language as well as your voice and eyes (plus a whole lot of heart) to witness to Jesus and his message.

Let us pray

Jesus, Master Catechist, please bless my voice, my eyes, my whole self, so that I may use these gifts to be your "sacrament," a sign of your presence to those I teach. Guide me and be with me as I share your message with joy. Amen.

For reflection and discussion

- If possible, ask someone to unobtrusively do a "home video" of you during one of your sessions. (Or, do a video of a "lesson" at home.) Watch the video to detect any signs of confusing or distracting body language (wandering, not keeping eye contact, nervous movements, monotonous voice, etc.). Make a simple plan to improve in that area.

- If you are teaching younger children (preschool to second grade) watch the adults on some of the TV shows for those age levels. How do the grownups use body language to emphasize/accompany their words? You don't need to imitate their style, but you can study how to use expression, eye contact, position, etc.

24

When You're Too Tired to Teach

Every catechist knows what it's like to feel too tired to teach. But what do you do? How do you get through in spite of what you feel?

Every catechist has at some time entered religion class feeling tired, hardly able to keep his or her eyes open, and walking around in a fog. I'm reminded of a cartoon I once saw of Garfield. He looked like the teacher I just described, and the caption read, "I will rise but I won't shine!"

You enter your teaching space. Your best self tells you you should smile. You can see the children hope you will. But all you want to do is get through this hour somehow. Now how can you change the water of this situation into wine? I'll admit that on a day like this you may not be able to get the best, sparkling wine, but I promise you, you can get wine! It's a matter of letting the Spirit take the lead.

The first step is prayer

I take it for granted that, as a catechist, you spend quality time outside of class in the company of the Master Catechist. You already know, then, that being thoroughly human, Jesus didn't always feel like teaching. At times he surely must have felt tired, overwhelmed, eager for some quiet time, wanting only to complete the task. He knows how it feels.

The first thing to do then is call out in prayer, "Jesus, help me!" That's all the prayer you'll need. Next look at the children because some of them will be smiling at you. Return the smile; it will loosen up your facial muscles.

Then make yourself think: "How lucky I am to be here! What a privilege to share in the work of Jesus, to tell these children about the kingdom!" This won't be easy but it can be done. I've tried it.

Begin with a song

Start your class with a lively song, one that the children really like. I've discovered that the more loudly children sing, the more enjoyment they get out of it, so encourage them to sing with gusto. If you can accompany the song with lively motions, all the better! You might even be able to have a procession while you are singing. Just have the children walk single-file in and out and around the free-standing furnishings, singing and clapping as they go.

You may want to use a tape or CD with your song on it. Then the burden of leading the song is not on you. (Incidentally, it's a great idea to keep tapes and CDs of favorite songs and hymns within easy reach—not only for when you're tired, but for when the children also are drooping, for whatever reason.)

Playing "Guess What?"

Another way to begin class on a "tired day" (or at any time) is by playing "Guess What?" which, as you've probably guessed, is a review tactic. Here's how it's done. Walk to the front of the class and just stand there for a few moments. Then say in an excited voice, "Guess what?" (Nothing gets our attention like the prospect of some new information.)

When the children call out "What?" you walk up to one child and say (for example), "I think we studied the Our Father in our last class. Right or wrong?" The child answers "Right!" or "Wrong!" If the answer is correct, heap on the praise. If the answer is incorrect, guide the child to the correct answer with leading questions. (There's never any reason for making a child feel like he/she failed, or to feel humiliated.)

The child who answered can ask the question, "Guess what?" and says to another child, "I think we covered _____, right?" The procedure continues until you call a halt, satisfied that the last class has been sufficiently reviewed. After you've used this technique several times, all you'll have to do is walk to the front of the room and stand still, and already you'll see children anticipating, "Guess What?"

Let me offer you just one more review tactic. Have the children open their books to the illustrations in the section you covered in your last lesson. Ask questions like these: "What's going on? Who are the people pictured here? What do you remember about our last class? What do these pictures have to do with the lesson?" Ask any questions that will involve your class in the subject at hand. This usually leads to some interesting answers, and you will soon know if the children got the point or not.

These few suggestions may lead to your own creative ideas for helping yourself on those "tired days." You may not be able to dance through that particular lesson, but you'll walk through it. And, hopefully, by the next session you'll once again feel happy and enthusiastic about your important role as catechist.

Let us pray

Jesus, I have no doubt there were days and times
when you were so tired you didn't want to teach.
One such time was when you crossed the lake
with your followers, looking for rest and quiet
after a long teaching day. But the people found

out where you were, and they arrived at your "hideout," excited, noisy, and eager for your words. You put aside your fatigue and lovingly taught them.

Jesus, when I feel tired, even before the session begins, please help me to follow your example. Amen.

For reflection and discussion

- Have you had "tired" teaching days? What did you do to help yourself complete the lesson? What worked? What didn't work?

- When you are feeling tired, tell yourself it's okay to feel tired; don't be tough on yourself. Then do what you can before class to perk yourself up: drink or eat something, take a quick walk, get some fresh air, take a quick nap.... If possible, start class with some quiet time so you can "catch your breath."

25

The Gifts of the Spirit

There are some very special graces that come to us catechists through the gifts of the Spirit: wisdom, understanding, counsel, fortitude, knowledge, piety, and fear of the Lord.

Wisdom

The first gift of the Spirit is wisdom, which we received at baptism, and which gives us the ability to love spiritual things. Spiritual realities like the sacraments, prayer, spiritual reading, and the corporal and spiritual works of mercy all have to do with discipline in one way or another because they help us develop our relationship with God.

How does this translate into discipline with your class? When a catechist is in regular contact with Jesus in the eucharist and through the other sacraments and spiritual helps, that catechist will take on the qualities and values of Jesus, will become wise in the ways of Jesus, and able to treat each child as unique and precious.

Another special benefit of the gift of wisdom is being able to judge rightly about persons, places, and events. We have two ways of judging: either from a purely secular viewpoint or from God's viewpoint. If we see children as persons placed in our life by God, how differently we will relate to them!

Understanding

The gift of understanding holds two particularly valuable treasures for us: 1) compassion and 2) the ability to distinguish what is important from what is unimportant.

Often these days, discipline problems are caused by children who are hurting, who have been affected by divorce, poverty, lack of food or proper medical care. Some children are emotionally and psychologically injured by a society fraught with violence and immorality. The gift of understanding makes us grateful that God has sent these children to us so we might try to give them the balm of healing that compassion can bring.

For catechists, knowing what's important and what's not is directly related to discipline. So often we forget that God has made us all unique and that some of us get to a goal one way and some in another. Yet often, in my own teaching career, I've insisted that all the children fit into the mold I've designed for them. Understanding helps us sift the essential from the nonessential, and accept the fact that the children in our classes are not all going to agree to act the way we have planned, and not all of them are going to accept our dictums unchallenged. This gift helps us respect a child's difference of opinion and discern what is important.

Counsel

The gift of counsel inspires us to pause in our hectic lives long enough to ask, "Lord, what would you have me do?" It is this gift that makes us yearn to hear God speaking to our hearts and minds, so we may be better prepared to share the Good News with the children in our classes.

The gift of counsel also helps us keep us from scattering our forces by flitting from one thing to another without any definite plan. It helps us slow down a bit when our rushing around affects us in negative ways. Another benefit of the gift of counsel is that it makes us willing to seek and grateful to receive the advice of others in our lives. What an enriching situation it is when each member of our team has the humility and sense to both seek and give good advice and suggestions.

Fortitude

Do you find yourself lacking in patience at times, wanting to take shortcuts like yelling at the children, segregating them, humiliating them? This is where the gift of fortitude comes in: it gives us patience in carrying out our duties. You can call on this gift, which we all received at baptism, to help you resolve tense situations.

For example, if a child is behaving in way that disrupts the class, you may with a little effort be able to turn that little "leader" in the right direction, by studying what his or her strategy is and training him/her to be your assistant when possible.

Another effect of the gift of fortitude is the courage to do what you have to do, and the good sense to know that you do not have to do everything alone. Just as we know that compassion is a great part of the technique of Jesus, we need to know that "tough love" is, too. Some catechists allow discipline in their classes to deteriorate because they either want to be popular with their children, or they are afraid of what people will think if they take a stand. But with many discipline situations (e.g., children using insulting racist language), only "tough love" action will work.

One source of help is from saints who were martyrs. The qualities they had are the very ones we need to handle difficult situations in our religion classes: resolve, courage, steadfast decisions, self-sacrifice, and the willingness to do what it takes to remain faithful to God. We can ask for their prayers and imitate their example in putting into practice the gift of fortitude.

Knowledge

The old saying that a little knowledge is a dangerous thing does not apply to the gift of knowledge given by the Spirit. With this gift of knowledge we can see more clearly what we need to change in our lives in order to grow in our relationship with God. This gift helps us see creation as the work of God, reflecting God's perfection. Knowledge also assures us that God gives us all the help we need to grow in love and to be with God forever.

Another effect of the gift of knowledge is that it helps us know what God expects of us. In a way, it's hard not to know what God expects; after all, God's Word is revealed all around us: in Scripture, in other people, in the commandments, in prayer. Doing what God asks of us is "another kettle of fish," however. We need to keep two things in mind: 1) the children already have the gift of knowledge through baptism and 2) God's presence is within and around them; it's just a matter of helping them be aware of it.

Piety

Though little understood by many of us, the gift of piety is a gold mine for good discipline. This gift helps us see ourselves as children of God and inspires us to turn to God often as to someone who loves us without measure. Piety helps us experience God's loving presence. It makes it possible for us to see God acting in our lives through other people. And piety enables us to address God in various ways.

All of these effects of piety not only guide us and help us grow personally, but also can direct our words and actions in our catechetical ministry. We can share our belief in God's love and loving presence with our children, and treat them accordingly.

Fear of the Lord

This gift also goes by the names holy fear, reverence, and respect. The gift of fear of the Lord helps us respect and reverence God and want to please God in whatever we do. It helps us "watch and pray" in moments of temptation and weakness. And this gift makes us more aware of God's holiness and gives us the desire to imitate it.

In our ministry, this gift will help us reverence God's presence in each child. It will also help us teach our children how to respect and reverence one another, and to imitate God who is holy and all-good.

Let us pray
Loving Holy Spirit, I thank and praise you for your presence and action in my life. Increase in me all your gifts so I may grow in love for God and for the children and families to whom I minister. Show me how to discipline as Jesus did, with love and respect for each child, created in God's image. Amen.

For reflection and discussion
- What place do the gifts of the Spirit have in your life? How do you see them as helping in your ministry? Do you feel that you are in need of a particular gift at this point in your work? Ask God for the grace to experience this gift.

- Sometime before Pentecost (or while teaching about the gifts of the Spirit), make a "gift of the Spirit" card for each child in your class. Outline a small bird figure, about three inches or so, on a piece of paper. Cut out the bird, and use it as a template to make copies on red paper, enough for all the students in your class. Next, write one of the gifts of the Spirit on the bird, alternating between all seven gifts. Cut out the birds, and give one to each child. Ask the children to try and live that gift throughout the year.

Of Related Interest

100 Fun Ways to Livelier Lessons
Maxine Inkel, SL

Refreshing, self-contained activities for children (grades 2-5) that offer catechists a wealth of quick, creative, flexible ways to observe holy days and holidays throughout the year.
0-89622-654-9, 128 pp, $14.95 (M-41)

100 Creative Teaching Techniques for Religion Teachers
Phyllis vos Wezeman

A wealth of practical possibilities for telling and reviewing the stories of Scripture and faith to their classes.
1-58595-141-2, 112 pp, $12.95 (J-89)

School Year Activities for Religion Classes
Gwen Costello

These creative "hands-on" activities are for every month of the school year and take just five to ten minutes. They can all be used to supplement almost any lesson in any textbook series.
1-58595-107-2, 64 pp, $7.95 (J-68)

Available at religious bookstores or from:

TWENTY-THIRD PUBLICATIONS
A Division of Bayard PO BOX 180 · MYSTIC, CT 06355
1-800-321-0411 · FAX: 1-800-572-0788 · E-MAIL: ttpubs@aol.com
www.twentythirdpublications.com
Call for a free catalog